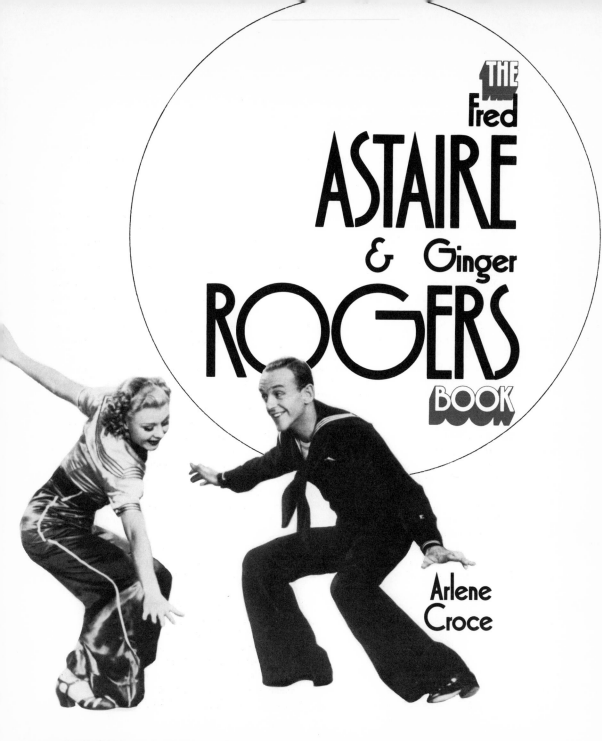

THE Fred ASTAIRE & Ginger ROGERS BOOK

Arlene Croce

OUTERBRIDGE & LAZARD, INC. NEW YORK DISTRIBUTED BY E.P. DUTTON & CO.

Standard Book Number: 0-87690-027-9
Library of Congress Catalog Number: 72-83107
Copyright © 1972 Arlene Croce
First published in the United States of America
in 1972. Printed in the United States of America.
All rights reserved including the right of reproduction
in whole or in part in any form.
DESIGN: LESTER GLASSNER

Outerbridge & Lazard, Inc.
200 West 72 Street New York 10023

Contents

FRED FLIPS OVER GINGER: In Shall We Dance, Fred Astaire as Petrov, star of the ballet, shows his scandalized producer Jeffrey Baird (Edward Everett Horton) a flip booklet of nightclub dancer Ginger Rogers in ''Rumba Ginger'' (above). PETROV: Isn't she lovely? BAIRD: Who is this girl? Where did you meet her? PETROV: I told you, I haven't even met her . . . but I'd kinda like to marry her. I think I will.

If you flip the pages of this book correctly, that is, with your left thumb from back to front, and with your right thumb from front to back, you will see a few seconds of Fred Astaire and Ginger Rogers dancing. The frames on the upper corners of the right-hand pages show them in The "Waltz in Swing Time" from *Swing Time*. Those on the upper left-hand corners are from "Let Yourself Go" in *Follow the Fleet*.

A Note on La Belle, La Perfectly Swell Romance

About four minutes into the movie *Shall We Dance*, Fred Astaire shows Edward Everett Horton a flip book of Ginger Rogers dancing and says, "I haven't even met her, but I'd kinda like to marry her," which is exactly what a movie audience of 1937 would have expected him to say. He's not just a man who has fallen in love with a picture of a girl, he's a man who has fallen in love with a girl who dances like *that*. From that moment on, the audience waits for them to dance together, knowing that Fred's feeling for Ginger can't be expressed in conventional love scenes—that until he dances with her he hasn't possessed her.

This very simple but very specialized form of love story was the basis of the series of Astaire–Rogers musicals that RKO produced in the Thirties and that many people regard as the greatest musicals in movie history. Certainly no greater dance musicals exist. Oddly enough, the dance emphasis that made them unusual also made them popular. Although Astaire and Rogers did many things in their movies besides dance—the way they looked and read their lines and wore their clothes and sang in their funny voices has become legendary, too, and they could make a song a hit without dancing to it—it was through their dancing that the public grew to love them and to identify their moods, the depth of their involvement, and the exquisite sexual harmony that made them not only the ideal dancing couple but the ideal romantic team. No dancers ever reached a wider public, and the stunning fact is that Astaire and Rogers, whose love scenes were their dances, became the most popular team the movies have ever known. In the three middle years of their partnership, they were listed among the top ten box office attractions in the poll of exhibitors conducted by *Motion Picture Herald*. In 1936, their peak year, they were in third place (after Shirley Temple and Clark Gable). It probably isn't a coincidence that their two films for 1936, *Follow the Fleet* and *Swing Time*, contain the best dances they ever did together. One can say of them, as of few performers in any art, that at their greatest they were most loved.

5

"Fred and Ginger," as we speak of them, are the characters created by Fred Astaire and Ginger Rogers while they are dancing. In their dance they grow suddenly large and important in a way that isn't given to Fred alone or to Fred with someone else. When Fred dances alone, he's perfect. For as long as we have known him he has been simply Astaire, *the* dancing man, self-defined. He is his own form of theater and we ask nothing more. But when he dances with Ginger we suddenly realize what further revelations that theater can produce: it can encompass the principle of complementarity. That principle has been missing from every Astaire film since his partnership with Rogers ended. He never ceased to dance wonderfully and he has had some good dancing partners. But it is a world of sun without a moon.

Ginger Rogers was, as a partner, a faithful reflection of everything that Astaire intended. She could even shed her own light. All of their great romantic duets took place, so to speak, in the light of the moon, and one of the pleasures of the RKO series is watching that lunar radiance increase. Rogers could never have won an international tap-dancing contest, but then she never tried. Her technique became exactly what she needed in order to dance with Fred Astaire, and, as no other woman in movies ever did, she created the feeling that stirs us so deeply when we see them together: Fred need not be alone.

Nor could Astaire have won an international tap-dancing contest, but who looks for mere technique from him? His "peerlessness" is a legend; it means, not that there were no other tap-dancers, but that there were no other Astaires. Above everything else, he was a master dramatist. Drama clings to every move he makes and to every move that Rogers makes with him. And yet they do not act, they dance. They had that kind of professional attitude toward, and respect for, dancing that comes from doing the work of it. At the core of their professionalism was a concentration upon dance as dance, not as acrobatics or sexy poses or self-expression. Their absorption gave plausible life and serious-ness to what remained generically lyric fantasy—the continuing lyric fantasy of which all their numbers were a part. Their confidence was such as to breed an almost mischievous gaiety. When they watch each other throughout the two duets in the "Continental" sequence of *The Gay Divorcee*, it seems impossible that the screen will ever again capture such a delicious *entre nous* sparkle of fun. To some observers the fun is a bit coldly technical; the dancing looks intricate and too objective, like the challenge of a competition ("Beautiful music . . . dan-gerous rhythm . . ."). Just as it should look, for in an Astaire–Rogers film the

dancing is often the only real, the only serious business. Their way of dancing up to a song, rather than down to a plot, is what takes you by surprise; that, and the way they give each song all the emotion that belongs to it, even if it is deeper than the plot and characterization allow for.

Yet the dances are not about nothing. Frequently they have the most intimate connection with literal plot action. The finale of *Shall We Dance* combines all the elements, symbolic as well as dramatic, of the plot. In "I'll Be Hard to Handle" in *Roberta*, they start the dance as casual friends and end it as soulmates on their way to love. The great "Never Gonna Dance" sequence recapitulates all the important action of *Swing Time* and sweeps it forward to a heart-rending climax as, in a spasm of clenched anger, she whirls out of his life. But while there is a great deal being said in these dances, Astaire never once changes his choreographic style. It stays very dry. Nor do he and Rogers ever press meanings upon us. Their smooth, informal, light objectivity continues straight across the lines of reference, and since the weight of gesture seems no more than what the music of the moment deserves, we are free to enjoy dancing unpressured by extraneousness, as audiences of the Thirties were free. And we may even feel like raising a silent toast to those audiences who could take their dancing, as it were, neat.

Those of us who were brought up on the movie musicals of the Forties and Fifties had much to enjoy: we had Astaire still, we had Garland, we had Gene Kelly, but we didn't have anything like the essential seriousness of the Astaire–Rogers movies. The major difference between Astaire and Kelly is a difference, not of talent or technique, but of levels of sophistication. On the face of it, Kelly looks the more sophisticated. Where Kelly has ideas, Astaire has steps. Where Kelly has smartly tailored, dramatically apt Comden and Green scripts, Astaire in the Thirties made do with formulas derived from nineteenth-century French farce. But the Kelly film is no longer a dance film. It's a story film with dances, as distinguished from a dance film with a story. When Fred and Ginger go into their dance, you see it as a distinct formal entity, even if it's been elaborately built up to in the script. In a Kelly film, the plot action and the musical set pieces preserve a smooth continuity of high spirits, so that the pressure in a dance number will often seem too low, the dance itself plebeian or folksy in order to "match up" with the rest of the picture. Wonderful as *Singin' in the Rain* is, the fun of it hasn't much to do with dancing.

The Astaire–Rogers dance films were romances, or rather, chapters in a

single epic romance. In a line from *Swing Time*, Dorothy Fields called it "la belle, la perfectly swell, romance." From *The Gay Divorcee*'s "Night and Day," the true beginning of the partnership, to "Never Gonna Dance," the last of the great romantic duets, it is only two years. But in those years dancing was transformed into a vehicle of serious emotion between a man and a woman. It never happened in movies again.

Prehistory

The romantic vision of dance that runs through the RKO series was no pretentious pose. Although it was conscious art, it came about, like so many "artistic" choices, through necessity. Astaire needed to establish himself as a screen star and hence as a romantic leading man. He has never thought much of himself as a straight actor and, at the time of his movie debut, he may have worried more than he had to about his age (thirty-four) and his looks. The list of male singers and dancers who have become big stars in the movies is very largely an assortment of aging, balding, skinny, tubby, jug-eared, pug-faced and generally unprepossessing men. Sound made it possible for actors like Chevalier, Astaire, Crosby, Dick Powell, Sinatra, Kelly and Lanza—all of whom became very big stars—to succeed on the strength of their personalities and on the special skills that projected their personalities. In sound films such men could play romantic leads rather than character parts. At the time of Astaire's entry into films, the seductiveness of sound hadn't been all that widely demonstrated; in quite a few cases—Ramon Novarro's, George M. Cohan's, Lawrence Tibbett's, arguably Al Jolson's—it hadn't revealed itself at all. In an interview with Cecilia Ager in 1934, Astaire talked about himself as "a sort of character actor" whom no one would believe if he said "I love you." He was about to prove, in *The Gay Divorcee*, that he didn't need to say it when he could sing or dance it, but at that time he was very much aware of the strikes against him. One of them was that he had never, even on the stage, really established himself as a romantic type. He had grown up in vaudeville, as one half of an act with his sister Adele, and in the public mind he was the lesser half. On Broadway he had asserted his independence in solo turns and in duets in which, through exigencies of casting, he was able to partner Marilyn Miller and Tilly Losch as well as Adele, but it was as Adele Astaire's brother that

8

he made his reputation, and, until she retired in 1932, he never did a show without her.

In the view of many who have watched his career develop, Adele was the best partner he has ever had. She was—contemporary opinion is unanimous on this point—a perfectly marvelous dancer, with a large share of the idiosyncratic Astaire charm. With her long slim legs, flashing smile and bold dark eyes, she was like a motto of the Twenties; the daffodil dresses and face-framing hats might have been created for her, and in her cooey soprano was something heartless, vague and self-adoring, the very cuckoo-note of a heedless era. Indisputably she was the first soubrette of the American musical stage, and hers was the style that shaped the material that made Fred and Adele Astaire a starring attraction. Together on Broadway they introduced "Oh Gee, Oh Gosh, Oh Golly" and "The Whichness of the Whatness" in *For Goodness Sake*, "How Do You Do, Katinka" in *The Bunch and Judy*, "Fascinating Rhythm," "Swiss Miss," and "I'd Rather Charleston" in *Lady Be Good*, "The Babbitt and the Bromide," "Funny Face," and "Let's Kiss and Make Up" in *Funny Face*, and "Hoops," "Sweet Music," and "White Heat" in *The Band Wagon*. The romantic ballads from these shows, like "The Man I Love" (from the original version of *Lady Be Good*), "He Loves and She Loves" and " 'S Wonderful" (from *Funny Face*), were generally performed by Adele with the show's other male lead. In *Smiles*, their worst flop, "Time On My Hands" had neither Astaire, and in *The Band Wagon*, a smash hit and their last show together, "Dancing in the Dark" was done by Albertina Rasch's dancing girls. (Astaire performed it years later with Cyd Charisse in the 1953 film *The Band Wagon*. In 1957 he did "He Loves and She Loves" and " 'S Wonderful" with Audrey Hepburn in *Funny Face*. Neither film bore any resemblance to the stage shows.) The Astaires rarely performed anything resembling a romantic adagio. Theirs was a comedy act, and even when they weren't cast as brother and sister, *l'amour* was unmistakably tongue-in-cheek.

Fred, of course, had droves of partisans during this period. He was a more than passable light comedian, a reliable singer, and in his dancing had already achieved the wizard-like perfection that, at least once an evening, could bring audiences to their feet. He was blithe and insouciant, perhaps a bit studiously so. Marshall and Jean Stearns, in their book *Jazz Dance*, trace his famous nonchalance to a defensive block he formed early against competing with his sister. "As he danced," they hypothesize, rather in the manner of amateur psycholo-

The Band Wagon, *Broadway, 1931: Adele and Fred Astaire, Tilly Losch, Frank Morgan and Helen Broderick.*

SAM S.
SHUBERT THEATRE

FRED ASTAIRE

GAY DIVORCE

Theater program, Broadway, 1932.

gists, "he gave the impression of thinking, 'Okay, Adele's the star, so I'll help her out, but I'm bored to death.' And, of course, it influenced the development of his style of dancing: the fine art of understatement." However he may have come by it, his casual, flip manner was the more affecting for being somewhat insecure. Beneath it all he had a pathos that could wring people's hearts. He was a Pierrot rather than a Harlequin. In *The Band Wagon* he had an off-beat triumph in a number called "The Beggar Waltz." He was the beggar, Tilly Losch was the ballerina. She tosses him a coin at the stage door. He sleeps and dreams he is her partner in the ballet. Two years later, when he opened in London in *Gay Divorce* (as the stage show was called), James Agate described Astaire's appeal as "a sublimated Barriesque projection of the Little Fellow with the Knuckles in his Eyes . . . every woman in the place was urgent to take to her chinchilla'd bosom this waif with the sad eyes and twinkling feet." This Astaire—the Astaire that less friendly critics tended to look upon as a lightweight juvenile charmer—is the Astaire that we see in his first films, *Dancing Lady* and *Flying Down to Rio*. He had magnificent aplomb but it was a callow, collegiate sort of aplomb. In *Dancing Lady* he looked a bit useless as Joan Crawford's partner; as Dolores del Rio's (in their tiny tango) he looked downright silly. Both ladies were too grand, too graciously accommodating; they underwent The Dance as if it were a purifying ordeal—they'd come out better women for having danced the first dance at the charity ball with the prizewinner. In Ginger Rogers Astaire met a kind of genial resistance. She

Gay Divorce, *Broadway, 1932: Fred Astaire and Claire Luce in "Night and Day." This was the only one of Cole Porter's songs that was used in the film version.*

brought out his toughness and also his true masculine gallantry, and so a new partnership was born and a career was saved.

For Astaire's career was imperilled when Adele left him. He had to prove he could sustain stardom on his own, and the first vehicle he chose, *Gay Divorce*, with music by Cole Porter, was very nearly a disaster. The *coup* of the show, however, was the dance he did with his leading lady, Claire Luce, to "Night and Day." Claire Luce was a languorous, sexy blonde who later went into straight roles (e.g. Curly's wife in *Of Mice and Men*). Astaire pays tribute to her in his autobiography *Steps in Time*: "Claire was a beautiful dancer and it was her style that suggested to me the whole pattern of the 'Night and Day' dance. This was something entirely different from anything Adele and I had done together. That was what I wanted, an entirely new dancing approach." "Night and Day" was, in fact, the first genuinely romantic adagio dance of his career. The significance of this wasn't much appreciated at the time—the novelty of seeing Fred without Adele was evidently too distract-ing—though most critics did single out the number as one of the two high spots of a generally dispirited show. (The other was a spectacular moment at the very end, when Astaire danced Claire Luce up onto the furniture and down again.) Astaire had taken a big chance, but instead of congratulating him on his success, the New York theater critics were pining after the girl who had married into the British aristocracy, never to return to show business. Adele was a persistent little ghost. It must have seemed to Astaire at the time that he would never succeed by himself on the New York stage that had been her playground.

There were two possibilities open to him. One was London, where the critics (as they proved when *Gay Divorce* opened there) were more sympa-thetic to his aims. The other was the movies. Each offered hope and heartbreak in about equal portions. London adored Adele, and it now had a proprietary interest, so to speak, in seeing her brother succeed. But the London theater, which had created musical comedy in the early years of the century, had lost its momentum by the Thirties. Nearly all the great show music was being com-posed by Americans for Broadway. What London did have was a reigning song-and-dance man, Jack Buchanan. Buchanan would have been no threat to Astaire in America, but competition in the relatively tight world of London musical comedy would not have been healthy for either of them. Besides, there was no one in America like Fred Astaire (or like the Fred Astaire to be); to

13

choose London would have been to choose retreat.

The movies. The advantage was that, incredible as it seems, Astaire was still unknown to movie audiences.* In 1928, when the first wave of movie musicals was just getting under way, he and Adele had been screen tested by Paramount for a film version of *Funny Face*. The test went the rounds. There is a cherished legend that it was seen by someone who passed the word on Fred: "Can't act. Can't sing. Balding. Can dance a little." Can anyone really have said that? There are Hollywood stories that one would like to discount simply because they're so "Hollywood." The industry in the late Twenties, however, was in a unique state of upheaval. In the rush to convert to sound, it was turning over on itself, trying in every obvious way to exploit sound before mastering the techniques that could make it expressive. The 1928 *Funny Face* never reached the screen, and a high percentage of the musicals that did certainly look as though they had been made by the man who uttered that rubbish about Astaire. It was a period of almost savage incompetence. If it seems to us unbelievable that the Astaires should have been passed over at a time when the movie-going public was about to be blitzed with musicals and the theaters were being raided for talent, it must also seem unlikely that their special gifts would have survived for long the primitive conditions and generally tasteless atmosphere of early sound film-making.

Early film musicals weren't equipped to record dancing of any complexity. They could and did record singers who could simply stand under the hot lights and sing. (When they raised their arms on a high note you saw the sweat stain underneath.) A performer usually did a number before the camera with a live orchestra on the sound stage. Retakes were expensive. The camera was enclosed in a booth to keep the sound of its motor from being picked up, and since it was forbidden to move the microphone as the performers moved, musical numbers took on a peculiarly cataleptic quality. You played, sang or danced to the mike, wherever it was. You did a nice little dance, and if you wanted the taps to register you didn't travel it far. Nothing too active or too ambitious. The camera didn't move much either. (René Clair at this time was moving both the camera and the microphone—but he wasn't doing it in Hollywood.) Legions of singers were launched in movie careers during the Stone

*Technically, Fred Astaire's movie debut occurred in 1915, when he and Adele appeared in the cast of a Mary Pickford feature called *Fanchon the Cricket*.

14

Broadway, 1930: Ginger Rogers in Girl Crazy.

Age of sound—Jeanette MacDonald, Maurice Chevalier, Al Jolson, John Boles, Helen Morgan, Dennis King, Grace Moore. They were helped by their stage reputations, and by radio, which had a tremendous effect on the pattern of American entertainment. Very few dancers of note appeared in feature films. Not only were they less well-known, they were too hard to integrate with the big static production numbers, too hard to get going in their specialties, too hard to cover if their specialties had no impact. Dancing was probably the one department that Hollywood, ravenous for novelty though it was, reserved pretty much for its own people. Movie stars who could sing were up against the new competition from Broadway and the airwaves, but movie stars who could "dance a little," like Nancy Carroll and Joan Crawford, and who didn't have to be placed for audience recognition, had a better time of it than stage headliners who were unfamiliar to the movie audience. It was charming to see Nancy Carroll dance—she was really very good—but neither Ann Pennington nor Marilyn Miller quite made it to movie stardom, and superb stage acts like the Four Covans, appearing in movies like *On With the Show*, literally got lost in the shuffle. The two-reelers of the period include some notable dance shorts. On a smaller scale and a lower budget, dancing was possible. But you didn't get to be a star in two-reelers.

Soon, to cut costs, the studios began filming to a piano accompaniment—the same piano to which the performers had rehearsed. Later on, an orchestral version of this track would be matched to the picture. It worked for everyone but the dancers. Cutting a dance sequence to the demands of exact synchronization was a totally unfamiliar task to film editors. The task was lightened if the dance movement was relatively simple in its relationship to the musical track. The technique of post-synchronization freed sound stages from the perils

of direct recording, but the separation of picture and sound introduced new perils in the cutting room, where a "down" dance accent would frequently be made to coincide with a musical upbeat. A rhythmically complicated dance presented hideous problems; in desperation, film cutters would cut away to crowd reactions, yapping dogs, gurgling babies—anything to avoid getting sight and sound together. (The practice survives, a kind of merry atavism, to this day.) As a consequence of this rough treatment, the level of film choreography dropped to below standard. Execution was even lower. Professional dancers weren't needed to perform mickey-mouse choreography and, until the studios started hiring music cutters, not many professional dancers applied. If it hadn't been for Fred Astaire, they might never have bothered with movies at all. Busby Berkeley, a Broadway choreographer under contract to Goldwyn, was already inventing ingenious ways to do without them.

Ginger Rogers, unlike Astaire, was well known to movie audiences, but she didn't become a star until the partnership with Astaire overtook and virtually remade her career. When she took the Claire Luce role in the movie version of *Gay Divorce*, not a few people thought she was miscast—it seemed so long since she'd been a lady. Actually, she had spent half her time in movies playing nice girls; and the other and better half playing wiseacres. It was the sharp and sassy Ginger that the public remembered. When, beginning with *Top Hat*, roles were written for her, the best of them combined the sharpness and the sensitivity. It was a unique combination.

She had started in vaudeville as a teenager, dancing, singing and doing patter routines composed by her mother, the indefatigable Lela. (Fred's mother, the almost equally indefatigable Anna Geilus Austerlitz, supervised his and Adele's career until Adele's retirement.) Movie appearances began in 1929, with shorts filmed in New York, and it was while she was performing in her first Broadway show that she made her first feature film at Paramount's studio on Long Island. The show was Kalmar and Ruby's *Top Speed*, the movie was *Young Man of Manhattan*, and she played the same kind of part in both: the babyfaced flapper with the piping voice and the "naughty" ideas. Hermes Pan, who would later become dance director of the Astaire–Rogers films, was also making his Broadway debut in *Top Speed*, in the singing chorus. The Ginger Rogers of 1929–1930, he recalls, was "the John Held Jr. Girl. She used to be billed that way in vaudeville, and it was her style at the time. She had those long John Held legs and real short, dark-red bobbed hair, and she used to sing sort of

ga-ga." The following season Rogers appeared as the lovelorn postmistress Molly Gray in the Gershwin show *Girl Crazy*. She sang "But Not For Me." (When MGM remade *Girl Crazy* in 1943, Judy Garland's name in the film was Ginger.) During rehearsals, Fred Astaire, who was opening the following month in *Smiles*, was called in to choreograph a dance to "Embraceable You" for Rogers and Allen Kearns. It was the kind of service he used to perform now and then for friends; he had once set a routine for Noel Coward and Gertrude Lawrence. On this occasion the friend in need was Alex Aarons, who had produced the Astaires' Gershwin shows, and so Astaire met Rogers for the first time. They became friendly and even dated a little, but Rogers longed to make movies full-time in Hollywood rather than part-time in New York.

When she arrived in Hollywood, she had no established persona. In *Young Man of Manhattan* in 1930, she had sung a typically kittenish number, "I've Got IT But IT Don't Do Me No Good." She was Clara Bow with just a dash of Helen Kane—she had in fact taken Helen Kane's place with the Paul Ash band in 1929—but the type was fading fast. When the Clara Bow image faded definitively into the Jean Harlow one, Rogers went blonde and made the transition from Twenties flapper to Thirties gold digger. By early 1933 she had found her form temporarily in the kind of parts that Joan Blondell and Glenda Farrell were also playing, but this time, instead of losing herself in the type, she wiggled around in it, trying to make it fit her. There has always been a strong element of precocity in the Rogers personality—something startlingly out of tune with her cutie face and figure—and when she makes her entrance in *42nd Street* with her monocle and Pekinese, or when she bursts into pig Latin in the middle of "We're in the Money" in *Gold Diggers of 1933*, the effect is almost eerie. She not only wears the monocle, she wears the Von Stroheim wince that goes with it. These were only shticks of course, but she made them seem original and disturbing. Astaire, when he came into movies, was already formed as a personality and as an artist, but movie audiences watched Ginger Rogers grow up. The bratty imitative cleverness that was so large a part of her talent sometimes got in her way, and she desperately needed polishing. In some of her early movies she even suggested a kind of junior Mae West but without Mae's all-consuming self-knowledge and control. She was a hot mama at the age of twenty-two. It was better than being a simple, straight ingénue, but it was a rotten fate for a clever child. Astaire would turn her into a goddess.

After the opening of *Gay Divorce*, Astaire asked the agent Leland Hay-

Dancing Lady, *Hollywood, 1933: Fred Astaire and Joan Crawford in* "Heigh Ho, The Gang's All Here."

ward to get him a job in pictures. Warner Brothers, the company that had started the rush to sound, had announced that musicals were coming back, had put *42nd Street*, a remake of *On With the Show*, into production, and had hired Berkeley away from Goldwyn to do the musical numbers. Hayward spoke to David O. Selznick, production head at Radio Pictures. Selznick mentioned that the studio was planning a big musical comeback with a picture called *Flying Down to Rio*. Selznick, however, was on the point of leaving RKO to go to work for MGM and could not have known much more about it. In the winter of 1933, there was not really very much to know. Like many Hollywood studios, Radio Pictures was in deep trouble financially. Organizationally it was in a state of confusion. Constant economy waves and the vacuum created by Selznick's resignation had left its leadership timid and indecisive. Besides, no one had much confidence in the market for musical films; even Warners was proceeding cautiously. But by summer the outlook was clear—everywhere except at RKO. One of Selznick's first productions at MGM (and his only musical) was *Dancing Lady*, starring Joan Crawford and Clark Gable, and introducing Fred Astaire. Selznick had expected to sign him for MGM, but when Astaire walked onto the *Dancing Lady* set he had an RKO contract in his pocket.

Despite the chaotic state of affairs at RKO, or perhaps because of it, Lou Brock, the producer of *Flying Down to Rio*, had got to Astaire first, and he may have managed it by offering him a leading role in a film that barely existed on paper. By the spring of 1933, Brock's plans were still tentative. In the RKO yearbook for 1933–1934, a lavishly appointed brochure announcing forthcoming attractions, there appears the first mention of *Flying Down to Rio*. Astaire heads the cast, which at this point consisted of Helen Broderick, who did not appear in the film, and Raul Roulien ("young Brazilian idol"), who did. In an interim book issued a few months later (and on the sheet music released in advance of the film), the billing reads: Dolores del Rio, Fred Astaire, Ginger Rogers, Gene Raymond and Raul Roulien. While RKO wondered what to do with its new property, the billing seesawed and the project turned into a starring vehicle for Dolores del Rio. She was to have one Aryan and one Latin lover, and Astaire and Rogers were to play supporting roles. In the end it was del Rio; then, in smaller print, Raymond, Roulien, Rogers, Astaire.

Astaire had hoped to enter pictures in a starring role. As a craftsman, he was determined to have control over the filming and cutting of his own numbers and he knew that nothing less than star status would give him that.

His contract with RKO, to which he says he "never gave a thought" at the time, was nothing special. From RKO's point of view it was virtually risk-proof. When the studio began fooling around with *Rio*, Astaire returned to his original idea, which had been to sell *Gay Divorce* to the movies. Mervyn LeRoy had seen the show early in its run and had mentioned it to Jack Warner, but Warner's answer—"Who am I going to put in it, Cagney?"—seemed typical of the attitude of Hollywood producers at that time. By an effort of the will (and by throwing the balcony of the theater open to cut-rate tickets), Astaire had pushed the show into a run of thirty-two weeks. This, in the desperately poor theater season of 1932–1933, was pretty good going. By March "Night and Day" was a best-seller. Still there were no takers.

Astaire tells the Jack Warner story in his autobiography and, although he writes about the period with a good deal of gentlemanly forbearance, it isn't hard to get the impression that 1933 was the most crucial year of his life. (He was also courting his first and only wife, Phyllis Potter, and he married her in July, just a few days before starting out in motion pictures.) Several years later, when his pictures were making millions for RKO, and MGM, with its *Broadway Melodies* and MacDonald–Eddy operettas, was running hard to keep up, people in Hollywood began wondering why, after having introduced Astaire at MGM, Selznick should have let his former studio grab him off. The truth is that Selznick was in no hurry to sign Astaire. He didn't think anyone else was either. He was right—and wrong. MGM had plenty of musical talent and RKO had only one rising young director, Mark Sandrich, who was interested in making musicals. It was Sandrich who pressed Brock to sign Astaire, and Sandrich was in a big hurry. But Sandrich then didn't have the authority to supervise Astaire's career and Brock was having his own problems. *Melody Cruise*, the first Brock–Sandrich feature musical, lit no fires under the public that had been stampeded by *42nd Street* and *Gold Diggers of 1933*. And the country was heading into the worst period of the Depression; the Radio-Keith-Orpheum Corporation had been in receivership since January. By July, when Astaire arrived in Hollywood and *Flying Down to Rio* still wasn't ready—but *Dancing Lady* was—the powers at RKO found it convenient to let him go to MGM for that one picture.

His role in *Dancing Lady* is a bit—a prestigious bit, but a bit. We wait an eternity for him to appear, and when he does—as himself (Gable, a director holding a rehearsal, calls out, "Oh, Fred, will you come here, please?")—he

Ginger Rogers (right) with Rudy Vallee and friends in Campus Sweethearts, *an RKO three-reeler, 1930.*

has two lines and then partners Joan Crawford in a run-through of the big number. After a few seconds, Joan gets a muscle cramp and Fred disappears until the end of the picture. The number is then seen. Actually, it is four numbers run together and Astaire appears in two of them: "Heigh-Ho, the Gang's All Here," an old Burton Lane–Harold Adamson song here given the white-tie-and-tails treatment, and "Let's Go Bavarian," which Lane and Adamson almost certainly dashed off with Astaire in mind, since it's an obvious pastiche of "I Love Louisa" from his show *The Band Wagon*. He doesn't get to do a solo and all too evidently was written into the picture at the last minute.

At the time probably no one thought that *Dancing Lady* would be remembered chiefly because it was Astaire's debut film. The talk was all of the labor troubles that were then hitting the lots (aggravating RKO's already harassed production schedules), and of whether it was the unions or Crawford who had stalled production on *Dancing Lady*. Crawford wanted Gable in the cast. It was presumably while waiting for Gable to become available that Selznick had the musical sequences in this film shot. Although later it would be said that he first signed Astaire and then dropped him (or, maliciously, that he deliberately "lost" Astaire as a slap at his father-in-law, Louis B. Mayer), Selznick might well have been glad to hire Astaire, RKO contractee though he was, and get on with *Dancing Lady*. Possibly, too, a few strings were pulled: John Hay Whitney, whose Pioneer Pictures had just been formed to distribute through RKO, was a good friend of both Selznick and Astaire. However matters stood with Astaire and Selznick and RKO, the *Dancing Lady* bit did what it was supposed to do for all concerned, and it provided an ideal fanfare for *Flying Down to Rio*, which was released a few weeks later. By the end of 1933, the RKO bosses knew what they had in Fred Astaire. Or possibly they knew a little beforehand, because they let him cut his own numbers.

21

Flying Down to Rio

An RKO Radio Picture released December 29, 1933

Executive Producer **Merian C. Cooper**   Associate Producer **Lou Brock**   Director **Thornton Freeland**   Associate Director **George Nicholls Jr.**   Screenplay **Cyril Hume, H. W. Hanemann** and **Erwin Gelsey**, from a play by **Anne Caldwell**, based on an original story by **Lou Brock**   Music **Vincent Youmans**   Lyrics **Edward Eliscu** and **Gus Kahn**   Musical Direction **Max Steiner**   Dance Direction **Dave Gould**   Photography **J. Roy Hunt**   Photographic Effects **Vern Walker**   Art Direction **Van Nest Polglase** and **Carroll Clark**   Costumes **Walter Plunkett**   Recording **P. J. Faulkner**   Editor **Jack Kitchin**   Sound Cutter **George Marsh**   Running Time 89 minutes

Songs: "Music Makes Me," "The Carioca," "Orchids in the Monlight," "Flying Down to Rio"

Dolores del Rio *Belinha De Rezende*   **Gene Raymond** *Roger Bond*   **Raul Roulien** *Julio Rubeiro*   **Ginger Rogers** *Honey Hale*   **Fred Astaire** *Fred Ayres*   **Blanche Friderici** *Titia*   **Walter Walker** *De Rezende*   **Etta Moten** *Singer*   **Roy D'Arcy, Maurice Black, Armand Kaliz** *Three Greeks*   **Paul Porcasi** *Mayor*   **Reginald Barlow** *Vianna the Banker*   **Eric Blore** *Butterbass*   **Franklin Pangborn** *Hammerstein*   **Luis Alberni** *Carioca Casino Manager*   **Jack Goode, Jack Rice, Eddie Borden** *Yankee Clippers*

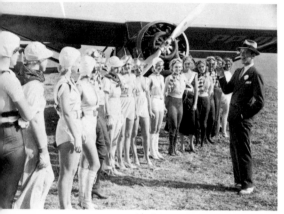

The Film. *Flying Down to Rio* is famous for Fred Astaire and the Carioca. For Astaire it was a triumph against all the odds. Fifth-billed, cast as long-suffering best friend, saddled with Herkimer Jerkimer lines like "Hold onto your hats, boys, here we go again" or an all-purpose "Yeah!" he nevertheless made an impression so strong that he could be ignored no longer. He arrived at a time when movies needed him most.

The Pioneer Period in movie musicals began in 1933. Producers in that year told themselves that with the onset of hard times the public wanted escapist entertainment. But a dull static musical is no more escapist than a documentary on breadlines. They were able to make musicals acceptable again because, technologically, the movies had advanced at a great rate. There was now a free and almost mad spirit in the musicals that began to come forth from the studios. It was a great period because material improvements were converted into a style; one might even say that for a time the improvements *were* the style.

The pioneer spirit fairly leaps off the screen in *Flying Down to Rio*. The plot is little more than pretext, and the movie was as hastily assembled as it looks. It's an Astaire–Rogers movie only in the sense that the two of them are in it—it really belongs to prehistory along with *Dancing Lady* and the twenty-odd films that Ginger Rogers made before it. But it is, in its own modest way, stupendous. It reverberates with the romance of modern communications, it crackles with technological pride. You get the feeling that its makers are testing the medium with an almost abstract delight in its possibilities.

In the Primitive Period (ca. 1928–1930) color had been introduced along with sound. Not until 1932 did Technicolor develop a three-color process that looked natural, but because it was expensive and cumbersome, the studios didn't revert to color photography when they went back to making musicals. (In the original prints of *Flying Down to Rio*, the scene of Raul Roulien singing "Orchids in the Moonlight" to Dolores del Rio was color-*tinted*.) Changes in film stock and lighting now allowed the use of white sets in sound films. As

Lewis Jacobs writes in his *The Rise of the American Film*, "previously white had been the worst color for the screen . . . because it had produced a dazzling effect; whenever white was wanted, pastel pink or green had been used instead." Cameramen like Sol Polito at Warners, Gregg Toland at Goldwyn, and J. Roy Hunt and David Abel at RKO exploited maximum contrasts in black and white photography to produce a rich visual mood for musical sequences. RKO went farther in this direction than any of the other studios. There, scenic designers Van Nest Polglase and Carroll Clark introduced the fixed architectural institution that soon became known as the B.W.S. (Big White Set). It appears in one form or another in nearly every Astaire–Rogers film: as the Carioca Casino, as the Brighton Beach esplanade in *The Gay Divorcee*, as Roberta's salon, and as Venice in *Top Hat*. Thereafter pieces of it turn up in various bandstands and stages until it reappears, much modified and subdued, as the country club in *Carefree*.

Hair and skin colors and textures, racial and ethnic types, were consistently and at times unfeelingly exploited. Could there have been an *aesthetic* reason why Ginger Rogers, invariably a blonde, always seems to have some lousy Latin lover at her side? In *Flying Down to Rio* "The Carioca" is sung in turn by a Caucasian, a mulatto and a Negro (Etta Moten, who had sung "Remember My Forgotten Man" in *Gold Diggers of 1933*), and danced by a white, and then a black, company. Brazil, with its racially mixed population, was a natural subject for the picture-makers in 1933. And to give it all heat, there's dusky Dolores del Rio, with her piano-key smile and black eye shadow, being crushed in the arms of white-blonde Gene Raymond in his silk aviator's scarf.

If Astaire seems to be playing an adolescent version of himself, it's because the studio couldn't think of new things for him to do—they gave him old things, or no things at all. As a member of Gene Raymond's band, he is equipped with an accordion, the instrument he played in *The Band Wagon*—only he doesn't play it here. He always seems to be stumbling into or out of awkward situations, and the sight of Dolores del Rio clearly terrifies him. He acts like somebody's brother. Not Ginger Rogers', though—and she isn't even somebody's girl. To anyone who knows the Astaire–Rogers films that followed, the lack of a relationship between them is most unsettling. Rogers might not have been in the film at all if Dorothy Jordan, who had been cast, hadn't decided to marry Merian C. Cooper, the head of the studio, and go off on a honeymoon rather than dance with Fred Astaire.

In their first movie, Astaire and Rogers were apart more than they were together. Left: "Music Makes Me" with Rogers and Gene Raymond. Right: Astaire sings the title number.

The Numbers. "Music Makes Me." Sung by Ginger Rogers as the band vocalist and reprised late in the film as background for a red-hot tap solo by Astaire. The peg for the number is in the lyric: Fred hears music, then he's through, 'cause music makes him do the things he never should do, i.e. steal the show.

"The Carioca." Sung by three ladies of Rio and danced by the chorus, with two frustratingly brief *entrées* by Astaire and Rogers. Their debut isn't terrific, only promising. Happily, the group dances are the best of any film in the series. The basic Carioca step is a to and fro tilt forehead to forehead and pelvis to pelvis, with the hands clasped overhead. The trick is for each partner to execute a complete turn without breaking head contact. It was suggested to Dave Gould by Hermes Pan, who was auditioning for a job as Gould's assistant. (Gould hired him.) Pan got the idea, as was customary in those days, from the words of the song: "Two heads together/ They say/ Are better than one/ Two heads together/ That's how/ The dance is begun." "The Carioca" was a fast tango similar to the Maxixe, which Vernon Castle had introduced to Americans

in 1914; he called it the "tango *Brésilienne*." The Maxixe never caught on, but strangely enough the Carioca did. People paid to have it taught to them in dance schools.

"Orchids in the Moonlight." The standard slumbrous tango, sung by Roulien to del Rio. A few inconclusive paces are then taken by del Rio with Astaire as the crowd gasps, "Look, Belinha is dancing our tango with an Americano!"

"Flying Down to Rio." Sung by Fred Astaire on the ground, whomped out by the RKO chorus and orchestra as the girls go by above. In 1926 Mildred Unger was filmed by Pathé newsreel cameramen as she danced the Charleston on top of an airplane 2,000 feet in the air. Wing-walking was a feature of every barn-storming flying circus of the Twenties. Although Dave Gould's girls were only a few feet above the ground, the sequence as it looks on the screen adds one element to Berkeleyan spectacle that Berkeley never thought of: terror.

Production. When Selznick left RKO he was succeeded for a brief period by Merian C. Cooper, the man who made *King Kong*. The advent of Merian Cooper has a direct bearing on the making of *Flying Down to Rio* in one sense; in another, it's not his kind of picture at all. Cooper was a journalist, an explorer and a former war pilot with a number of business interests, chiefly movies and aviation. He wasn't much more interested in making musicals than Selznick had been, but someone at RKO had taken the command decision to get back into musicals. Lou Brock, with Mark Sandrich directing, had produced an Oscar-winning musical short subject in 1932 called *So This is Harris*, and followed it with a feature, *Melody Cruise*, again starring Phil Harris, and containing an iceboat ballet (white sails, black ice) created by Dave Gould, who was of the Busby Berkeley school. Now Brock proposed to go all out in an effort to smash Berkeley off the screen. He managed to sell Cooper on the idea by combining two themes close to Cooper's heart—aviation and South America. The setting would be Rio de Janeiro and the film would climax in an aerial circus. Cooper was a member of the board of directors of Pan American Airways, which in 1932 had opened the first air express service from Miami to the principal coast cities of South America. The clipper ships that Sikorsky designed for Pan Am are in the film, adding a throbbing excitement to the film's promise of a Rio "where the lovely Brazilian ladies will catch your eye/ By the light of a million stars in the evening sky." Whether or not the picture promoted passenger air travel to South America, it was full of splendid visual themes.

Task force of "The Carioca."

Relying on what turned out to be excellent back-projection and process shots, the studio sent a camera crew to Rio to collect background footage. The finale, with girls festooning the wings of planes as they fly over Rio Bay (partially dubbed by Malibu Beach), was shot in a hangar with a few planes hung from the ceiling and some wind machines. In order to cut overhead, Thornton Freeland and George Nicholls Jr., working with separate units, shot the film in four weeks. Freeland had directed two of the better early musicals, Goldwyn–United Artists' *Whoopee* and United Artists' *Be Yourself*, with Fanny Brice. Nicholls was an RKO hand. Vincent Youmans, whose jeweled score set the mood for the entire film, was ill with tuberculosis while writing it. It was·his second original film score and virtually the last creative work of his life. After completing it, he retired to a Denver sanatorium, where he died in 1946.

Another bit of helpful self-publicity was the line in the title tune that goes "send a radio to Rio de Janeiro," i.e. a radiogram. Del Rio and Raymond are seen sending wires to Rio in the film, courtesy of RCA Communications Inc. The RKO Corporation was an affiliate of RCA and shared with it ownership of the Radio City Music Hall. It is thought that the theater's operating deficits in the first months of the Depression were what drove RKO into receivership. The new theater wasn't built for film exhibition, but a few weeks after it opened during Christmas week of 1932, it became a permanent film showcase with booking guaranteed for the big RKO films. *Flying Down to Rio* was the Christmas attraction in 1933, by which time an end to receivership was foreseen. The Astaire–Rogers films kept RKO afloat during the next few years. Prophetically, the fadeout of *Rio* isn't on its stars but on Fred Astaire and Ginger Rogers.

The Gay Divorcee

An RKO Radio Picture released October 12, 1934

Producer **Pandro S. Berman**   Director **Mark Sandrich**   Screenplay **George Marion Jr., Dorothy Yost** and **Edward Kaufman,** from *Gay Divorce*, book by **Dwight Taylor,** musical adaptation by **Kenneth Webb** and **Samuel Hoffenstein**   Production Associate **Zion Myers**   Musical Direction **Max Steiner** Dance Ensembles Staged by **Dave Gould** Photography **David Abel**   Photographic Effects **Vernon Walker**   Art Direction **Van Nest Polglase** and **Carroll Clark**   Costumes **Walter Plunkett**   Music Recording **Murray Spivack** and **P. J. Faulkner Jr.**   Recording **Hugh McDowell Jr.**   Editor **William Hamilton**   Sound Cutter **George Marsh**   Running Time 107 minutes

Songs: "Night and Day" (music and lyric by **Cole Porter**), "The Continental" and "A Needle in a Haystack" (music by **Con Conrad**, lyrics by **Herb Magidson**), "Don't Let It Bother You" and "Let's K-nock K-neez" (music by **Harry Revel**, lyrics by **Mack Gordon**)

Fred Astaire *Guy Holden*   **Ginger Rogers** *Mimi Glossop*   **Alice Brady** *Hortense Ditherwell*
Edward Everett Horton *Egbert Fitzgerald*   **Erik Rhodes** *Rodolfo Tonetti*   **Eric Blore** *Waiter*   **Lillian Miles** *Hotel Guest*   **Charles Coleman** *Valet*   **William Austin** *Cyril Glossop*
Betty Grable *Hotel Guest*   **Paul Porcasi** *Nightclub Proprietor*   **E. E. Clive** *Customs Inspector*

The Film. When one considers that only ten minutes out of the total running time of *The Gay Divorcee* are taken up by the dancing of Astaire alone or with Rogers, the film's enduring popularity seems more than ever a tribute to the power of what those minutes contain. For their first co-starring film, the studio surrounded Astaire and Rogers with a great deal of "protective" tissue—a lot of clowning by Edward Everett Horton, the incessant Alice Brady, and two more farceurs brought in from the stage production, Erik Rhodes and Eric Blore. There are songs and dances by other performers than the stars, and there's a great giddy whirligig of a production number. It all falls away in retrospect.

Most people don't realize how short dance numbers are, even on the stage, and how hard it is to sustain one for more than three minutes, which was Astaire's average length. The general complaint about all the Astaire–Rogers films is that there's not enough dancing. It seems so because the rest of the film is dull by comparison—what wouldn't be dull by comparison? The dances are poetry; even the best prose of which RKO was capable can't console us for what seem wasted minutes. Although later on there would be more numbers, the proportions established in *The Gay Divorcee* remained basic to every Astaire–Rogers picture.

What is more damaging to a film like *The Gay Divorcee* is the gap in taste between the story and dialogue portions, and the numbers contributed by Astaire. One grows eventually fond of the stale comedy routines and of the earnest, good-hearted and often very talented people employed to perform them. But one's first reaction is that the two stars have somehow fallen among a gang of mental incompetents, and that includes the people behind the scenes writing the script. Much has been written about the character relationships in the Astaire–Rogers films—about how Fred and Edward Everett Horton are bachelor buddies until Ginger, a wise but wary girl, takes the advice of her confidante, usually Helen Broderick, and lets Fred calm her suspicions—or something of the sort. But that story is told, or rather implied, in only a few of the films and even then it is not the whole story. In the first six films they

made together. Astaire and Rogers alternated between playing the couple who carry the romantic interest and the couple who provide "relief," comic or otherwise. The two-couples formula was standard to musical comedy, and the model script for the series was *Flying Down to Rio*. Sometimes, as in *The Gay Divorcee*, the other couple would be older, but when Astaire and Rogers were not the serious pair of lovers, the other pair would be the same age. The male friendship theme was standard, too, and scriptwriters of the Thirties had their kicks with it. A male star was supported by a comic, and it's surprising in how many musical comedies and operettas of the Twenties effeminacy was a comic's stock-in-trade. In *The Gay Divorcee*, which had a retrogressive book, all the male comics seem queer. The title was changed to take the edge off that hard word "divorce." Perhaps something should have been done about the adjective.

The Numbers. "Don't Let It Bother You." Sung by showgirls in a Paris nightclub and played again when the proprietor forces Astaire to dance for his dinner. Not as important as:

"A Needle in a Haystack," the number that first defined the Astaire character on the screen. Here he is, thumping on the mantelpiece, testing the floor, vaulting the sofa, and generally behaving as if his mind were on anything but going out to search the streets for the girl of his dreams. In Astaire's own words, he was "a guy who's got it made." The miraculously casual low-key delivery, the elegance of his handling of props (the dressing gown which he tosses behind his back, with a slight hitch and a double-take, at his valet), tell us that he's omnipotent. Everything comes easily to him, and we believe in him as in no screen hero since Keaton. Astaire had done a getting-dressed-and-going-out routine to "New Sun in the Sky" in *The Band Wagon*. Here he demonstrates that screen choreography could consist of a man dancing alone in his living room.

"Let's K-nock K-neez." Must we? A number inspired by a routine in the stage show for G. P. Huntley Jr. and some bathing beauties. Here staged by Hermes Pan for Edward Everett Horton in wrinkled shorts and Betty Grable in the same satin lounging pajamas worn by Dolores del Rio in *Flying Down to Rio*. Horton's best partner was Eric Blore. Later in the film they have a contest to see who can do the most takes on a single line.

"Night and Day." This incomparable dance of seduction is a movie in itself.

Left and above: "Night and Day."

They're alone in a ballroom. It is night with an ocean park in the background. Abruptly she turns and crosses the set; he blocks her. She crosses back and he blocks her. She turns away, he catches her wrist, their eyes meet and he dances ingratiatingly. Again she turns, again he catches her and she walks into the dance. When she stands away, he pulls her by the hand and she coils against him, wrapping herself in her own arm, and the free hand holds that wrist. In this position, together as if cradled, they just drift. . .

Astaire adapted his stage choreography, and no more thrilling or more musical dance had ever been presented on the screen. The song was already a classic; to watch it danced almost forty years later is to hear it for the first time. Like all great choreographers, Astaire frequently works against the music. The steps are in perfect counterpoint, and the tension builds like a dramatic undertow. There is one extraordinary occurrence: the moment when she makes a sudden decision and strolls away from him. (Rogers never walks, she always strolls.) When he approaches, she appears to strike him, and he staggers back slipfooted the length of the stage. Mysteriously, the moment is on the same level with everything else—it's a *dance* moment and it tells us much about Astaire and Rogers. They never break their stride. They don't act when they should be dancing.

Rogers at this point in the series dances a little stiffly and she loses her line in her turns. But her style is brilliant and she knows exactly what she's doing. The wonderful ending is all her: the way she gazes up wordlessly at this marvelous man she's been dancing with exalts him, her, and everything we've just seen.

"The Continental." Sung by Ginger Rogers, Erik Rhodes, and Lillian Miles. Danced by Astaire and Rogers and a cast of perhaps not quite one hundred,

on the "futuristic" esplanade at the Brightbourne Hotel. Ads for *The Gay Divorcee* billed Astaire and Rogers as "The King and Queen of Carioca." This was the follow-up, and how it chunters on: new variations, new camera angles, new armies of dancers trotting forward, couples in black, couples in white, girls in black, boys in white, then girls and boys in black and white blite and whack together. Yet there's method in it: something interminable in the music—a half-note vamping phrase (D, D flat, C, C sharp) that loops the end of the song into the beginning—connects with something in the imagery of the production: the whirling of shadows on a wall, the motion up and down a staircase, the slow turning of revolving doors in which clusters of girls are braced, turning, like figures on medieval clocks. Time without end in "The Continental."

Mark Sandrich disliked numbers that were entirely closed off from the plot, so he and Dave Gould arranged to break up "The Continental" with plot continuity. They got the stars into the number by having Astaire stick a paper silhouette of himself and Rogers onto a phonograph turntable, throwing a shadow on the wall that makes their jailer, Rhodes, think they are in the next room dancing. The naiveté of the device is offset by its perfection as a subliminal motif in the number, and while the music goes round and round, Sandrich builds suspense by cutting away to Rhodes and those whirling shadows. The suspense is heightened when Rhodes emerges with his concertina to sing a chorus. Sandrich also cuts away to a dance bit by Eric Blore.

Gould's staging of the dances has a theme-and-variations plot but no continuity within the dance structure. He merely cuts, dissolves or flash-pans from one formation to the next, and Pan's ensembles in "The Piccolino" follow the same procedure. There was no excitement in the permutations to compare with the unfolding logic—or the surrealistic illogic—of Busby Berkeley's numbers at Warners (*cf.* the inexorable "Lullaby of Broadway" in *Gold Diggers of 1935*). Nevertheless, "The Continental" keeps going compulsively in a kind of delirium all its own. When, after about ten minutes, Lillian Miles sings a whole new verse reeling off all the countries where they do the Continental, we recognize the cue for Astaire and Rogers to go into their Spanish bit, their Hungarian bit, their Viennese waltz bit, and finally, into the jazz Continental. Astaire follows the lyric's direction to "kiss while you're dancing" by kissing Rogers—on the hand—and so on. It's very cleverly worked out and the whole business runs 17½ minutes, a record length then and for some time to come. Only in Thirties

musicals do we dream like this.

"The Continental," waltz reprise. Up, over the furniture and down again, *à deux.* They dance up, he swings her down. Dancing on the furniture is Astaire's own motif in this film. Only in Astaire musicals do we dream like this.

Production. Lou Brock, the man most directly responsible for bringing Astaire to Hollywood and for teaming him with Ginger Rogers, lost control of the star package when Pandro S. Berman took over as acting head of production at RKO. On Brock's schedule after *Flying Down to Rio* were *Hips Hips Hooray* and *Cockeyed Cavaliers*, with Bert Wheeler and Robert Woolsey (who were then a top-grossing RKO team), and *The Great American Harem*, with Skeets Gallagher and Pert Kelton. H. N. Swanson, another RKO producer, was put in charge of the film that was announced as the first Astaire–Rogers co-starring vehicle, *Radio City Revels.* (RKO was still in a self-publicizing mood.) At about the same time, negotiations were begun for the rights to *Gay Divorce*, which Astaire was then doing in London, and Berman suggested to Brock that he consider producing it as the follow-up to *Radio City Revels.* As Berman tells it, Brock said, "I can blow a better script than that out of my nose." With Merian Cooper's return, Berman left for Europe on a vacation. In London he saw *Gay Divorce* and thought, "My God, Lou Brock is crazy." In February of 1934, Berman returned from vacation having bought the show for $20,000, which was low even then. Brock meanwhile had developed a script from a story by himself and Herbert Fields about some madcap socialites stranded in the South Seas. It was called *Down to Their Last Yacht* and Berman couldn't see where Astaire and Rogers would fit into it. He decided to produce *Gay Divorce* himself. The trade press carried a story that he tried to get Roy del Ruth from Fox to direct, but that del Ruth's price was too high. Cooper then took a long leave of absence in Honolulu to recuperate from a heart attack, and Berman, resuming control of the studio, assigned Zion Myers to supervise the production. Myers was a cousin of Mark Sandrich, whom Brock had been keeping busy on the Wheeler–Woolsey features.

Down to Their Last Yacht, with Mary Boland, Polly Moran and Ned Sparks, opened to poor notices (though it didn't do badly at the box office), and Brock's contract was not renewed. In 1935 he was at 20th Century Fox, in 1940 he returned to his old job at RKO as head of the shorts department, and subsequently

produced B pictures for different studios. He died in 1971 after many years in obscurity, and his last job was as a night clerk in a Hollywood hotel.

About *Gay Divorce* Brock wasn't necessarily crazy. Its book was a throwback to the old Princess Theater musicals. Dwight Taylor, who wrote the play on which Samuel Hoffenstein and Kenneth Webb based their libretto, and who had nothing to do with the musical version in either stage or screen form, had taken his plot from an unproduced play by his step-father, J. Hartley Manners, called an *An Adorable Adventure*. Its archaisms were retained in the musical. Astaire played a writer of cheap novels who meets a girl in London, loses her, and finds her at a Brighton resort (called Brightbourne in the film), where she mistakes him for the hired co-respondent in her divorce suit. In the transition from stage to screen, Astaire's profession was changed to dancing, the asinine lawyer friend played by G. P. Huntley Jr. was broadened to fit Edward Everett Horton's great bumbler, and Luella Gear's role as Hortense, a droll creature of some asperity, was recast as a feminine version of Horton's. Alice Brady, a distinguished and versatile actress (she was Lavinia in the Theatre Guild's production of *Mourning Becomes Electra*), had had a hit the year before as the effusive society matron in the film of *When Ladies Meet*. Like Horton, she became typed. Out of type (as in *Young Mr. Lincoln*) she is almost unrecognizable. The character of Tonetti the co-respondent was changed, too. In the play he chased girls; in the film he's a harmless cuckold. The finale of the stage show paired Guy and Mimi, Hortense and Tonetti, and Egbert and Barbara, a bathing beauty who survived vestigially in the film, and is played by Betty Grable.

Two contract writers, Dorothy Yost and Edward Kaufman, worked on the screenplay, with Kaufman supplying new gags for Horton and Rhodes. In May, Myers put George Marion Jr. on it, whom Berman had hired from Paramount to write *Radio City Revels*. Marion had worked on *Love Me Tonight* in 1932; so had Samuel Hoffenstein, the co-librettist of *Gay Divorce*. The resemblance between the Astaire–Rogers courtship and the Chevalier–MacDonald one probably is not accidental. It was Lorenz Hart who wrote "Mimi" for Chevalier. Did he take this very singable name out of Cole Porter's (and Astaire's) mouth?

After *The Gay Divorcee*, Mark Sandrich went on to direct four more Astaire–Rogers films. He was born in New York and trained as a physicist. As a director he retained a methodical, efficiency-engineering cast of mind, although his personality was warm and excitable. Carmel Myers, the silent film star,

was another cousin. (She was Zion's sister.) One day while visiting one of her sets, Sandrich solved an electrical problem for the crew and soon found himself working as an assistant prop man. Eventually he began directing, with two-reel comedies at Century, and in 1930 he joined Lou Brock's shorts department at RKO as a specialist in comedy.

Sandrich was wowed by the possibilities of film musicals. *So This Is Harris*, his Academy Award-winning three-reeler, was one of the first films to reflect the developments in technique that made the second phase of musicals possible. Sandrich had done a great deal to perfect the playback (the method of filming the action to a prerecorded sound track), although, in the Astaire–Rogers series, some of the relatively simple numbers that involved singing, such as Astaire's solos, would continue for a time to be directly recorded on the set. Nowhere in the series does one see people singing *while* dancing, and without losing breath; the only blatant falsity is the dummy orchestras one sees playing on the screen—six- or eight-piece ensembles blaring forth with the power of a symphonic band. This was perpetrated to avoid paying a full complement of musicians for film appearances and also, one feels, to preserve the line of the B.W.S. And, of course, it was an early sound gag.

On *The Gay Divorcee*, the basic Astaire–Rogers production unit began to assemble. There were Sandrich and David Abel, the cameraman, and other such invaluable and uncredited persons as Argyle Nelson, the assistant director; Ben Holmes, the dialogue director; and Trudy Wellman, Sandrich's secretary and script girl. Sandrich also worked closely with Dave Gould on the conception of "The Continental," and Hermes Pan was the link between Astaire, who worked apart, and Sandrich–Gould. Pan, also uncredited at this time, did the bulk of the group choreography for the film, while Gould "staged" it, i.e. devised the ideas and planned the camera angles. Gould's star fell as Pan's rose. Astaire wasn't interested in competing with Busby Berkeley; he was Berkeley's opposite. In 1935 Gould went to MGM, where he won an Oscar for an Eleanor Powell number and the Straw Hat number in Fox's *Folies Bergère*.

In 1934 Ginger Rogers had seven pictures in release. Except for *The Gay Divorcee* only one of them was a musical, *Twenty Million Sweethearts*, with Dick Powell, a dull satire on radio which she did on loan-out to First National. RKO had promised Rogers diversified roles and now it was announcing her for every Fred Astaire project it could think of. In March, she filed suit against radio

"Other couple" trouble: Edward Everett Horton and Alice Brady.

station KFI, NBC's San Francisco affiliate, for broadcasting an interview in which a person purporting to be Ginger Rogers admitted that she couldn't do dramatic roles as well as musical comedy ones, and promised to eat more Health Bread. Rogers' lawyers found that the program's hostess, a self-styled expert who gave the stars advice that was generally in line with what the studios wanted of them, had had RKO's permission for the impersonation. Ironically, Astaire hadn't wanted Rogers in *The Gay Divorcee*; he felt she would be wrong as the refined English girl, and his experience after Adele's departure made him fearful of becoming part of another team. The studio, with the public's happy connivance, quashed this rebellion right at the start. The box office spoke, and it spoke of the impending professional marriage of Rogers and Astaire. Sheer chance had thrown them together in "The Carioca," but, as they say in *The Gay Divorcee*, "chance is the fool's name for fate."

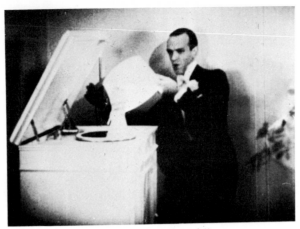

Above and next page: "The Continental."

In 1934 the studio still considered Rogers a featured player—not yet a star. In *The Gay Divorcee* it gave a number to Betty Grable, a contract player not yet a featured player. Grable couldn't handle dialogue at this point in her career, and in *Follow the Fleet* she was back to playing a bit. Lillian Miles, who sings in "The Continental," was a Wampas Baby Star in the same year as Ginger Rogers (1932), and was being personally coached by Al Siegel, whose big find had been Ethel Merman. There was a massive campaign to popularize the Continental as a ballroom dance *à la* the Carioca. Eight chapters outlining and illustrating the movements were released to newspapers as "Dave Gould's Eight Easy Lessons." Unlike the Carioca, the Continental had no dance gimmick and was show dancing besides. It didn't go very far, but the song won the first Academy Award for Best Song, and the film started a fad for Venetian blinds.

In 1938 RKO released a film called *Radio City Revels* that had nothing to do with the abandoned Astaire–Rogers project. The stars were Milton Berle, Jack Oakie, Victor Moore and Helen Broderick.

Roberta

An RKO Radio Picture released March 8, 1935

Producer **Pandro S. Berman**   Director **William A. Seiter**   Screenplay **Jane Murfin**, **Sam Mintz** and **Allan Scott**, with additional dialogue by **Glenn Tryon**, from the play *Roberta*, book by **Otto Harbach** based on **Alice Duer Miller**'s novel *Gowns by Roberta* Music **Jerome Kern**   Production Associate **Zion Myers**   Musical Direction **Max Steiner**   Dances **Fred Astaire**   Assistant Dance Director **Hermes Pan**   Photography **Edward Cronjager**   Art Director **Van Nest Polglase**   Associate Art Director **Carroll Clark**   Set Dressing **Thomas K. Little**   Gowns **Bernard Newman**   Music Recording **P. J. Faulkner Jr.**   Recording **John Tribby**   Editor **William Hamilton**   Sound Cutter **George Marsh**   Running Time 105 minutes

Songs: "Let's Begin," "Yesterdays," "Smoke Gets in Your Eyes" (lyrics by **Otto Harbach**), "I'll Be Hard to Handle" (lyric by **Bernard Dougall**), "I Won't Dance" (lyric by **Oscar Hammerstein II**, screen version by **Dorothy Fields** and **Jimmy McHugh**), "Lovely to Look At" (lyric by **Dorothy Fields** and **Jimmy McHugh**)

Irene Dunne *Stephanie*   **Fred Astaire** *Huck Haines*   **Ginger Rogers** *Scharwenka* **Randolph Scott** *John Kent*   **Helen Westley** *Roberta*   **Claire Dodd** *Sophie*   **Victor Varconi** *Ladislaw*   **Luis Alberni** *Voyda*   **Ferdinand Munier** *Lord Delves*   **Torben Meyer** *Albert*   **Adrian Rosley** *Professor*   **Bodil Rosing** *Fernande*   **Johnny (Candy) Candido**, **Muzzy Marcellino**, **Gene Sheldon**, **Howard Lally**, **William Carey**, **Paul McLarind**, **Hal Borne**, **Charles Sharp**, **Ivan Dow**, **Phil Cuthbert**, **Delmon Davis** and **William Dunn** *The Wabash Indianians*

The Film. Out of circulation since the early Forties and never shown on television, *Roberta* is the least known and least discussed of the Astaire–Rogers films. Because they share billing with Irene Dunne, a legend has grown that it's a minor and unrepresentative film. On the contrary: it's a key film. It widens their range and establishes them unshakeably as a team. Astaire and Rogers become Astaire–Rogers in this film—you can see it happening.

It's true that the roles they play are inflated supporting roles, but since none of the characters has much definition and the story makes very little sense, this doesn't diminish their impact. It lets them soar. *Roberta* gives us that soaring spirit in such abundance that, in a way, it does stand apart from the rest of the series. It's their most ebullient film.

There may have been a special reason for the ebullience. *Roberta* was being filmed while the returns from *The Gay Divorcee* were rolling in and the RKO lot was rocking with success. The Astaire–Rogers portions of the film are charged with a kind of excitement unusual even for them. Audiences at *The Gay Divorcee* were breaking out in applause, and in *Roberta* there is space at the end of all their numbers for applause, led by the audience in the film. Because they weren't burdened with the need to carry a plot, the Astaire and Rogers roles were easy to build up with the kind of custom-tailored material that makes them more vivid than those of Dunne and Scott. Scharwenka and Huck seem to be the most spontaneous characters in the film, while Stephanie and John are caught in the machinery of a plot that has stopped moving.

Not that it had ever moved very far. The uneventful libretto of the stage show was criticized at the time, and many reviewers seemed mistrustful of a musical that could end in a fashion show, as if that were a kind of cop-out. A musical fashion show was not a new idea; it was the old Follies showgirl parade in couturier terms and had been done at least as early as 1919, in the "Alice Blue Gown" show, *Irene*. Maybe 1919 and not 1933 was the proper period for *Roberta*. Otto Harbach's story source was a trifling piece of blueblood fiction, one of those novels in which people have no character, only station. It translated well into operetta, and the setting—*emigré* Paris with its White Russian colony—appealed musically and perhaps emotionally to Jerome Kern. But a show which has as its climax a football player quarreling with a Russian princess (in disguise) over the cut of a gown? To dilute the tea rose atmosphere Harbach threw in an American jazz band and a comedian, Bob Hope. But *Roberta* remained

genteel nostalgia, nebulously evocative and a little quaint. Its songs are imperishably beautiful; mainly, however, it was the film version, with its unrepeatable star cast, that caused the show to survive longer than Kern's other "continental" operettas of the same period, *The Cat and the Fiddle* and *Music in the Air*, both filmed once (in 1933 and 1934 respectively) and forgotten. The vitalizing presence of Astaire and Rogers converted *Roberta* from continental operetta to American musical comedy, and the film paved the way for *Swing Time*. *Roberta*, in versions more or less faithful to the film, is periodically, and always haplessly, revived. Bob Hope has done it twice on television, and in 1952, MGM made it as *Lovely to Look At*, with Howard Keel, and with Kathryn Grayson feverish as Irene Dunne, and Marge and Gower Champion suicidal as Rogers and Astaire.

The Numbers. "Let's Begin." Performed on the steps of Roberta's salon in Paris by Huck Haines and his band, the Wabash Indianians, because there's a rich Polish countess upstairs who might get them a job. During the routine the countess trucks on over to the window and Huck recognizes Lizzie Gatz, his old girlfriend from Indiana. "Let's Begin" has bits by Candy Candido, the trick-voiced comic who made "Ah'm feelin' mighty low" a catchphrase in the Forties, and Gene Sheldon, the banjoist who was even then getting his finger caught in the strings. Earlier, the Indianians had auditioned for the proprietor of the Café Russe by doing the Pipe Organ: Huck plays on their outstretched hands, gloved to resemble organ keys, and they groan in harmony. Lizzie gets them a job—at the Café Russe—where she sings as the Countess Scharwenka because "you have to have a title to croon over here."

"I'll Be Hard to Handle." This is the big event of the film, the number in which "Fred and Ginger" became fixed screen deities. The wonderful secret they seemed to share in "The Continental" becomes here a magical rapport that is sustained through three minutes of what looks like sheerest improvisation. It begins with some light banter punctuated by dance breaks, continues with music and more dance breaks—a tap conversation with each taking eight-bar "sentences" (his growing more impudent, hers more indignant)—and ends in a chain of turns across the floor and a flop into two chairs. The context for the number is an informal session on the dance floor of the Café Russe, the audience for it consists of bartenders and cleaning women, and the beauty of it is that it really seems to be happening for the first time—it's like a moment

The Wabash Indianians do The Pipe Organ.

of *cinéma vérité* bursting through the surface of a polished commercial film. We've all seen numbers in musicals that start in this supercasual way—and the "impromptu" walked-right-into number became a staple of the Astaire–Rogers repertory—but how many times, no matter how good the routine or how sophisticated our response, it happens that we feel a little stab in our childish hearts—"Oh, they've rehearsed." Sanity tells us that Astaire and Rogers have rehearsed; publicity statistics tell us how many back-breaking hours. But the difference between them and other performers is that, watching them, we aren't in possession of our sanity, we're happy children again, the story the number tells us is true. And the illusion of spontaneity makes the plot implication of the number credible; it cements the relationship of the screen characters they portray.

In the stage show the song was special material for Lyda Roberti, the Polish-Hungarian bombshell. Ginger Rogers, singing in a thick accent, parodies Roberti's scat style and mannerisms hilariously in one of the great wacky-Ginger routines (like "We're in the Money" and the Swedish bit in *Bachelor Mother*).

"Yesterdays." Mme Roberta is really Minnie, an American. Years ago she ran away to Paris and made her fortune as a dressmaker. Now she is sung to sleep every afternoon by Stephanie, her head designer, who is really a Russian princess. (Half the principals in the stage show were in disguise; the film adds one more, Rogers' Lizzie-Scharwenka.) Irene Dunne sings two lullabies in the film. One is a lovely Russian folk song inserted by Kern, and the other, on the day of Minnie's death, is "Yesterdays." In the stage show, Fay Templeton as Minnie sang it on her deathbed, and the film follows the original setting for it exactly, with the light dying as Dunne sings the last measures. At the

48

"I'll Be Hard to Handle." Rogers' two basic costumes were backless evening gowns and pants. This was the first of the numbers in pants.

end of the song—very beautifully sung to a simple guitar accompaniment—there is a slow dissolve and an orchestral reprise begins, continuing under the bulletin of Roberta's death and culminating in an outpouring of Tchaikovskyan sentiment as Dunne stands motionless in the empty room.

"I Won't Dance." The incredible Astaire plays several choruses of what he calls in the film "feelthy piano"; then, as the band jams away, Rogers shimmies into the shot, wearing a lamé gown that sets off her hair and figure, and sings to him provocatively: "When you dance you're charming and you're gentle/ 'Specially when you do the Continental"—and the orchestra quotes a few notes

from their last film. But this doesn't sway him. Two big Cossacks have to carry him protesting onto the dance floor, and there he does his longest and most absorbing solo of the series so far, full of stork-legged steps on toe, wheeling pirouettes in which he seems to be winding one leg around the other, and those ratcheting tap clusters that fall like loose change from his pockets.

"Smoke Gets in Your Eyes." Balalaikas play for the lyric highlight of the film, sung by Dunne in her tiara to a tableful of sentimental Russians at the Café Russe. The words were supposedly based on a Russian proverb, "When your heart's on fire, smoke gets in your eyes," and in the course of the scene there's an acrimonious plot exchange with Randolph Scott, who indeed has flown away by the time Dunne takes up the release. Later on in the film there's a dance reprise, the first formal romantic adagio to be created by Astaire for himself and Rogers—and for the beautiful supple back that let her arch from his arms like a black lily. The dance is almost humble in its brevity and simplicity—a few walking steps, a sudden plunge, a silky recovery, and it's over. But the spell that blooms while you are watching it is powerful, and there are astonishing moments, like his very tender gesture of pressing her head to his shoulder as they walk.

"Lovely to Look At." For the fashion show in the film Kern wrote this pretty, fluttery, feminine tune sung by a luminous Irene Dunne, commencing with the seldom-heard verse about the effect of a lovely gown on the heart of a man. A pity the dresses designed for the film are ugly to look at. (The audience applauds in relief when Rogers emerges in her simple bias-cut black satin.) Lucille Ball appears as one of the models.

"I Won't Dance" reprise. Seconds before the fadeout the film gives us one last satisfying glimpse of Astaire and Rogers, destiny's tots, before they go on to make the film that was now being prepared especially for them under the title Irving Berlin had given it—*Top Hat*.

Production. On the way to London to see *Gay Divorce* in December 1933, Pandro Berman had stopped in New York and seen *Roberta*. A few months later Radio bought it for $65,000, outbidding Paramount and MGM. Irene Dunne was announced for the role played on the stage by Tamara. It was Berman's idea that Astaire would play a combination of the roles done by Bob Hope and George Murphy (who had the part of a hoofer with the band in the show, the California Collegians); and Rogers would play a version of Lyda Roberti's

role. It was to be a double-romance type plot. New material would have to be written. Jane Murfin, the author of *Smilin' Through* and a top writer for RKO's women stars (Constance Bennett, Ann Harding, Irene Dunne), adapted Otto Harbach's libretto. A writer of comedy material, Sam Mintz, was assigned, and then another, the former actor Glenn Tryon. While Mark Sandrich was preparing *Top Hat*, Berman assigned an old friend, William A. Seiter, to direct *Roberta*. Seiter had directed, or rather, unleashed Rogers in *Professional Sweetheart*, one of her best pre-Astaire performances, and in *Chance At Heaven* and *Rafter Romance*. Allan Scott, who describes his contribution to *Roberta* as "a brush-over," remembers Seiter as a jolly man who laughed all the time: "I don't know how he ever directed." Seiter was a sympathetic hack. His direction of *Roberta* is relaxed to the point of passivity, but it isn't cold, and its permissiveness didn't extend to the slack timing of comic dialogue that was Sandrich's major flaw.

Only about a third of the original score of *Roberta* came to the screen. Following what remained for years customary procedure in the filming of Broadway shows, RKO commissioned new songs for its stars. It also elected to cast Randolph Scott, a non-singer, and Victor Varconi, a singer who doesn't get a chance to sing, as the two men in Dunne's life. ("The Touch of Your Hand," Stephanie's duet with Ladislaw, is background music in the movie, as is "You're Devastating.") Jerome Kern's collaborators on the new material were the team of Dorothy Fields and Jimmy McHugh, who had supplied many songs for motion pictures, among them the title number of *Dancing Lady*. "I Won't Dance" was not written for Astaire but adapted for him by Fields and McHugh. It had been introduced the previous spring by Adele Dixon in a London show called *Three Sisters*, produced by Kern and Oscar Hammerstein II and starring Charlotte Greenwood. The revised lyric has become standard.

In the "I Won't Dance" number, Fred Astaire plays a hot two-piano arrangement with an off-camera partner. It was Hal Borne, who was one of the Wabash Indianians in the film. Borne played a bigger role in life; he was Astaire's rehearsal pianist on all the RKO films and, along with Hermes Pan (who receives his first screen credit on *Roberta*), contributed creatively to the arrangements of the dances.

In the search for starring vehicles for Astaire and Rogers, RKO seems to have been initially seduced by the trend to continental raffishness and romance epitomized in the Lubitsch and Mamoulian movies with Maurice Chevalier and Jeanette MacDonald. Nothing would have been worse for Astaire and Rogers

than *Ringstrasse*, a play about a Viennese cloakroom attendant and a high-spirited young girl who gets him in trouble with her underground pals. The studio purchased it early in 1934 from its author, the Hungarian playwright Aladar Laszlo, one of whose works had been the basis of *Trouble in Paradise*, the brilliant Lubitsch film of 1932, starring Kay Francis, Herbert Marshall and Miriam Hopkins. *Ringstrasse*, suitably adapted to the American scene, was supposed to follow *The Gay Divorcee*, and there is some evidence that when Jerome Kern resettled himself in Hollywood in 1934, he was given *Ringstrasse* to work on. Among the copyrights taken out by Kern in 1935 is an unpublished composition called "Dream of a Ladies' Cloakroom Attendant," and copyright was renewed on another Kern song, "Vienna." Mysteriously, the studio had changed Laszlo's title to *The World By the Tail*; another mystery is what it proposed to do to "Americanize" the play—the screen treatment by Allan Scott suggests nothing so much as Melchior Lengyel *mit schlag*. Luckily, Kern and RKO chose the Americanization of *Roberta* instead. If they hadn't, the Astaire–Rogers series might have taken an altogether different turn.

Astaire and Rogers played loose kibitzing roles in the plot of **Roberta**. When they aren't giving advice to their co-stars, they're blazing up the screen with their dances. Left: "I Won't Dance." Left below: With Irene Dunne. Right below: "Smoke Gets in Your Eyes."

Top Hat

An RKO Radio Picture released September 6, 1935

Producer **Pandro S. Berman**   Director **Mark Sandrich**   Story **Dwight Taylor**
Screenplay **Dwight Taylor** and **Allan Scott**   Music and Lyrics **Irving Berlin**   Musical
Direction **Max Steiner**   Ensembles Staged by **Hermes Pan**   Photography **David Abel**
Photographic Effects **Vernon L. Walker**   Art Director **Van Nest Polglase**   Associate
Art Director **Carroll Clark**   Set Dressing **Thomas K. Little**   Gowns **Bernard Newman**
Music Recording **P. J. Faulkner Jr.**   Recording **Hugh McDowell Jr.**   Editor **William
Hamilton**   Sound Cutter **George Marsh**   Running Time 101 minutes

Songs: "No Strings," "Isn't This a Lovely Day (To Be Caught in the Rain)?" "Top Hat,
White Tie and Tails," "Cheek to Cheek," "The Piccolino"

Fred Astaire *Jerry Travers*   **Ginger Rogers** *Dale Tremont*   **Edward Everett Horton** *Horace
Hardwick*   **Erik Rhodes** *Alberto Beddini*   **Eric Blore** *Bates*   **Helen Broderick** *Madge Hard-
wick*   **Edgar Norton** *London Hotel Manager*   **Gino Corrado** *Venice Hotel Manager*
Leonard Mudie *Flower Salesman*   **Lucille Ball** *Flower Clerk*

The Film. Tentatively in the late Thirties and then defiantly in the Forties and Fifties the musical was democratized. What had been an art form for experts who needed no excuse to sing or dance became a mass ritual. The lyric impulse was pandemic and therefore its own justification. It was the era of the naturalistic musical, of folksy outings in the country with everyone singing as they packed their steamer rugs and picnic baskets, or of people arriving in New York or Paris with their legs planted far apart. Seeing *Top Hat* for the first time in the early Fifties was like seeing a film made in ancient Egypt. It had stylization on top of stylization. The plot and settings and manners and clothes established one level of artifice, and balanced on top of that were perfect cut-glass flowerings of dance and song that rose to infinite heights.

Contemporary reviews of *Top Hat* praised its spontaneity, its smooth integration of plot and musical numbers. That was what its makers worked for and, if the results, to a later generation, seem supererogatory it's because the whole film starts from a non-literal premise. In the class-conscious Thirties, it was possible to imagine characters who spent their lives in evening dress—to imagine them as faintly preposterous holdovers from the Twenties, slipping from their satin beds at twilight, dancing the night away and then stumbling, top-hatted and ermine-tangled, out of speakeasies at dawn. It was a dead image, a faded cartoon of the pre-Crash, pre-Roosevelt Prohibition era, but it was the only image of luxury that most people believed in, and *Top Hat* revived it as a corrected vision of elegance. Unlike William Powell and Myrna Loy in *The Thin Man*, Astaire and Rogers in *Top Hat* are decorous, and when Helen Broderick orders a drink at the Lido it's a "horse's neck," an innocuous glass of ginger ale with a lemon peel unfurled from brim to bottom. *Top Hat* is a Thirties' romance of the Twenties, the sins of the decade wiped clean by a flow of lyrical optimism, all innocence regained in the exhilaration of "stepping out, my dear, to breathe an atmosphere that simply reeks of class," as the title song puts it. *Top Hat* is essentially an innocent film; its satire (of continental manners, of Venice as a kind of celestial powder room) is semi-wish-fulfillment.

Of all the Astaire–Rogers films *Top Hat* and *Swing Time* come closest to

Eric Blore in consternation. The top Astaire-Rogers supporting player, he appeared in five of their films.

the level of the magnificent numbers they contain. The first hour of *Top Hat* is unqualified joy; only after "Cheek to Cheek" does the film drop off into a desert of talk, and "The Piccolino" is too late and too short to revive our wilted spirits. The script is not dull, but Mark Sandrich seems more gifted as a technician of musicals than as a director. For all his stop-watch discipline he had a faulty sense of pace in the construction of a scene. The actors' takes are too long and too broad, and the lines are read as if they were by Congreve. Both Astaire and Rogers, as actors, have a rapid inner tempo; the film doesn't adjust to this, it enforces a stately rhythm throughout. Yet this does let actors like Horton and Blore and Rhodes—and Broderick, in her over-sane, island-of-calm way—register with all their might. Full-fleshed caricature (rather than character) acting is a lost art; at least I had always thought so until I noticed that Rhodes' Tonetti-Beddini had a real-life modern-day counterpart in Enzo Stuarti. Perhaps what is lost is the time-sense that allows Blore to give a line like "*Sic transit gloria mundi*, sir" its full rococo spread; and something that seems to go with it, an air of *dolce far niente* purposelessness, which in 1935 was ludicrous and enviable at the same time.

The Numbers. "No Strings (I'm Fancy Free")." Songs don't have to be worked into a plot to be effective, and this song, and the dances that Astaire does to it, are engaging enough to stand on their own, but the sequence that was built around the routine is a classic of its kind. *Top Hat* gives us Astaire in the best role ever written for a dancer in a movie; the dance technique is an element in the characterization. Jerry Travers is literally footloose, he's bumptious, he's a disturber of the peace. At the beginning of the movie he offends the members of a stuffy London men's club by crackling his newspaper. On the threshold he delivers a parting salvo of taps. A few minutes later, in the hotel suite, he launches his song in the middle of a sentence: "In me you see a youth who's completely on the loose. No yens, no yearning, *no strings, and no connections* . . . , and the exuberant dance he breaks into explodes upon the midnight hour. We watch just long enough to get excited about what's

Below: ''No Strings.''

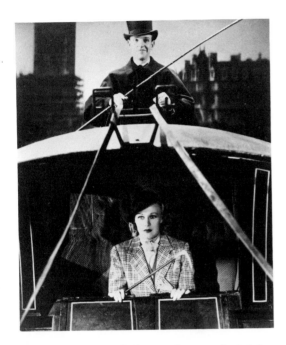

coming next, and then a boom shot takes us to Ginger Rogers in the room below, rising from her satin pillows like an angry naiad from the foam. It was by now customary for Astaire–Rogers romances to begin with him annoying her, but *Top Hat* accomplishes this without the undue bitterness of *The Gay Divorcee*'s skirt-tearing scene, and with a song—one that makes their meeting sweetly ironic. Both song and dance swerve to a halt when he catches sight of her standing grimly in the doorway. "Every once in a while I suddenly find myself dancing," he says with complete plausibility, and she retorts, "I suppose it's some kind of affliction." After she leaves, the music goes into a *diminuendo* reprise, but the number keeps on climbing. He sprinkles sand on the floor—"I've appointed myself her official sandman"—and, in the movie's sexiest scene, dances on it with caressive little strokes as she snuggles back to sleep. Jerry Travers' tap-dancing feet are the film's *leitmotiv*: they tap on the box of the hansom cab to let Dale Tremont know that she's his prisoner; tapping again on the ceiling of the Lido hotel room, they spring the plot onto its homeward course. And they are, of course, a kind of mating call that leads

her to join him in the most enchanting number in the film:

"Isn't This a Lovely Day?" From the shooting script: "The thunder is really a tympani effect and the lightning is a *glissando* which starts the music." Is there anywhere in movies more wonderful thunder and lightning? Rain numbers are always fun, but what could match that *second* clap of thunder that shifts the rhythm into double time, or the moment when we see the bandstand through

60

the rain and the whirling pair alone on their private stage? Basically, this duet is a challenge dance (he does a step, she copies it, he does another, she tops it, and so on) and, like the tap conversation in "I'll Be Hard to Handle," was a common form of tap duet. But there is nothing common about the way these dances are executed, and their freshness has nothing to do with the lexicon of tap technique. For those who care about such things, Astaire put on a tap-

dancing exhibition with Eleanor Powell in *Broadway Melody of 1940*. In the duets with Rogers, who was a less proficient technician but a much more appealing performer, the point isn't tap-dancing, it's romance. And in "Lovely Day" every step has the dewiness of fresh, young emotion. Those spurting little phrases that end in a mutual freeze (when the music stops, starts and stops again on uneven counts) as if to say "try and catch me," and that ecstatic embrace, when they pivot together in a wide circle all around the stage, whipping it into a froth—if this isn't perfect dancing, it is the perfect joy that dancing like this aims for and a shining moment in the history of the musical film.

"Top Hat, White Tie and Tails." In the Ziegfeld show of 1930, *Smiles*, Astaire had done a number called "Say, Young Man of Manhattan" (coincidentally also the title, without the "Say," of Ginger Rogers' first feature film) in which he danced in a top hat against a line of men in top hats and then shot them down one by one with his cane. *Smiles* flopped, but Astaire was fond of the number, and four years later he told Sandrich that he would like to try it again in movies. The result, to one of Berlin's most rhythmically inventive compositions, is an Astaire classic, and though the choreography was designed for the theater it's a movie classic too. Astaire's imagination turned a straightforward song-and-dance routine with a male chorus into something dramatically suggestive, with a touch of gangsterism. There's a *"misterioso"* passage in which, the chorus having momentarily disappeared, the lighting and music are lowered and he reacts to unseen presences like a man being threatened on a lonely street. Like the "rebuff" in "Night and Day," it is pantomime that looks like dancing—you may not even be aware of any special intent, and the meaning of the passage is nonspecific. All one can say about it is that it seems intrinsically related to the big "shooting gallery" mime routine that follows, and that no one but Astaire would have thought of it.

"Cheek to Cheek." For me, the high point of this most famous of all Astaire-Rogers numbers is the singing of the song, which comes before the dance. It's a long song (64 measures) with a motion as regular as breathing, offset by little bursts of syncopation, and with one unexpected departure (the "Dance with me!" section) like a full-voice exclamation that blazes once in the midst of a whispered conversation and then drops with a sigh. A truly transporting song—and lyric: "The charm about you/Will carry me thru to/Heaven . . ." and so it does, in the long take that holds on them while we listen.

"Top Hat, White Tie and Tails."

"Cheek to Cheek." Dancing with the man she thinks is her best friend's husband, Ginger is appalled by Broderick's signal of "Go on, get together." "Well, if Madge doesn't care, I certainly don't," she says. "Neither do I," replies Fred. "All I know is that it's Heaven . . . I'm in Heaven. . . ." Wearing the most famous of all her dance dresses (ice-blue satin with feathers galore), Ginger is led to a secluded spot somewhere in Venice.

Astaire's face is peculiarly beautiful when he sings; the strain of his features when he hits the difficult notes (and there are quite a few in this score) gives him an intense look of romantic ardor. And Rogers is perhaps never more beautiful than when she's just listening; she never takes her eyes off him and throughout this scene I don't think she changes her expression once. The modesty of the effect makes her look like an angel: such a compliant, unasking attitude, handsome beyond expectation in such a fierce woman. She also wears a maidenly kind of hairdo unusual for her, and a most becoming makeup. While we drink all of this in, they're dancing farther and farther away from the crowd, just normal fox-trot dancing in medium shot, until, at the conclusion of the song, an orchestral crescendo takes them over a bridge, onto a balcony and into the big dance. It's a good number, very much on the model of "Smoke Gets in Your Eyes," and there are several dreamy backbends for Rogers, but the dance is a bit ritzy, a bit too consciously "poised"; and the dramatic action—the grand seduction—has already occurred.

"The Piccolino." Unlike "The Carioca" and "The Continental," which were extended compositions allowing plenty of room for a big production number, "The Piccolino" is a concise romp in 2/4 time that creates a feeling of spaciousness by moving wildly through a series of key changes. Moreover, the lyric deals not with a dance but with a song. As production numbers go, "The Piccolino" is not devastating and probably wasn't meant to be. The sensation that Astaire could produce dancing by himself or with Rogers in unadorned settings had pretty well killed the public's fancy for monster spectacles and, at least as far as RKO was concerned, this was to be the last of them.

It's a friendly medium-size monster with a sense of humor. "The Piccolino" is satire, and Berlin's lyric kids the whole process of the big exotic production number by coming right out and admitting its phony origin: "It was written by a Latin / A gondolier who sat in / His home out in Brooklyn / And gazed at the stars." The set designers kidded themselves in the same spirit, and the only loss is that the film as released doesn't convey the extent of their creation.

It's frustrating, too, to be given the wonderful Astaire–Rogers duet without an encore. (After all, they did dance twice in "The Continental" and twice, if fleetingly each time, in "The Carioca.") The Astaire–Rogers "Piccolino" is a scintillating, dipsy-doodle affair in which they literally kick up their heels. Rogers is especially fine in it, and she also sings the song.

66

Production. Astaire on Broadway had worked in shows by Kern and Gershwin and Youmans and Porter, but he had never done an Irving Berlin show, and Berlin had not since 1930 done a complete film score. In November of 1934, while *Roberta* was in production, Berlin was signed by Berman and Sandrich for two Astaire films. In their first exchange of ideas, Sandrich told Berlin about the "Young Man of Manhattan" number that Astaire wanted particularly to do, and perhaps under the spell of the greatest routines Astaire had done so far—the getting-dressed-and-going-out routines in *The Band Wagon* and *The Gay Divorcee*—Berlin wrote, "I'm puttin' on my top hat, tyin' up my white tie, brushin' off my tails . . . ," rhyming "tails" with "I just got an invitation through the mails." Berlin, who could not read or write music notation and picked out his tunes on a specially built piano that transposed keys automatically, always needed someone to make his piano parts. Hal Borne remembers working nights with him at the Beverly Wilshire Hotel. "Berlin went 'Heaven—' and I went *dah-dah-dee*, 'I'm in heaven—' (*dah-dah-dee*). He said, 'I love it, put it down.' " Then, after several more conferences with Astaire, Sandrich and the writer Dwight Taylor, a spring starting date was set for the film, which was to be called *Top Hat*, and Berlin flew back to New York.

It was Taylor's task to devise an original screenplay, working into it the numbers that Berlin had written so far and suggesting ideas for further ones. By Christmas he had completed a treatment, and in it is the "No Strings" sequence, much as it was to appear in the finished film. In a British film of 1934, *Evergreen*, Jessie Matthews had done a charming impromptu solo in a handsome duplex apartment, to Rodgers and Hart's "Dancing on the Ceiling," but the number failed to dramatize the action described in the lyric. Taylor introduces Ginger Rogers by having Astaire wake her up as he tap-dances in the room above, and then has him put her to sleep again with the sand-dance. It is all there in the treatment, right down to the piece of plaster that falls as she's telephoning.

Next, Taylor has Astaire driving Rogers in the hansom cab to the riding stables in Hyde Park. They go to the zoo and here, Taylor brightly suggests, "a musical novelty number may be introduced: 'In the Birdhouse at the Zoo' . . . 'If I can, you can—so can the Toucan do what two can do' . . . 'You'll not be heard but we'll get the bird in the birdhouse at the zoo.' " Still inventing, Taylor thinks that there might be music from a bandstand a moment later,

striking up Berlin's "Wild About You," with perhaps a reprise on a carousel. In Taylor's first rough draft continuity, with dialogue and stage directions, there's no zoo or carousel, and "Wild About You" is still there, but by this time it's raining in the park, and Rogers, soaked, is taking refuge on the band-stand where Astaire sits, insolently cracking peanuts. He pushes back the tar-paulin that covers the piano and manages to make himself agreeable by singing the song, and then they dance. "Wild About You," copyrighted 1934, remained in the script of *Top Hat* for a month. Berlin did not use it until *Louisiana Purchase*. (When it was dropped from *Top Hat*, the piano and the peanuts went too.)

The transition to the Lido in Venice, in Taylor's treatment, called for a beach routine by bathing girls and continental types passing in review, with "perhaps a patter chorus by Helen Broderick which she does so well." The "Top Hat" number is spotted late in the film as the big production number, introduced with Astaire's getting an invitation to attend a party at the Lido Palace. Wrote Taylor: "We go into the 'Top Hat, White Tie and Tails' number as our characters prepare for the festivities and maintain the number on a LAP DISSOLVE into the party itself." By the end of January, this number had become what it is in the film, Astaire's single in the London theater before the switch in locale. He goes on just having received Broderick's invitation to join her and Rogers in Venice. Besides "No Strings," the only number that seems to have fit right from the start is "Cheek to Cheek," occurring about two-thirds of the way through the action, with Broderick bringing Astaire and Rogers together on the dance floor at the Lido restaurant. This is the big romantic duet of the film, but in the first version of the script there was another and even starrier one later on, to a song called "You're the Cause," which Berlin apparently never published. This duet was to have been danced along the quay by moonlight, and the setting and emotions that Taylor suggests for it seem to have been transferred to the "Cheek to Cheek" dance we see in the film. "You're the Cause" ended with the ride in the gondola that Astaire and Rogers take in the film (with Blore as the gondolier getting left behind), and Taylor wanted them to spend the night together floating on the bay, a very anti-Code idea.

There's a lot of *The Gay Divorcee* in *Top Hat*, enough to qualify it as a remake. The hinge of the plot is a mistaken-identity mechanism, and its link to *The Gay Divorcee* is obvious. Here Taylor, who had written the play *Gay Divorce*,

was rewriting himself, but with one tiny difference that has caused an inordinate amount of confusion over the authorship of *Top Hat*. Once more, the name of Aladar Laszlo crops up. At about the time that he sold *Ringstrasse* to RKO, he also sold it a play written by himself and Alexander Farago, called *A Scandal in Budapest*. The studio had Karl Noti adapt it to the screen and in the fall of 1934 tried to get it cleared by the Hays office. Back came a bill of particulars headed: "We would remind you that illicit love and illegitimacy are not proper subjects for comedy." The only thing that Taylor took from the Laszlo–Farago play was the incident in which Rogers, seeing Astaire carrying Horton's briefcase, thinks he must be Horton, i.e. the husband of her best friend. In the Hungarian play it was a violin case (the hero was a violinist). In no other way does *Top Hat* resemble *A Scandal in Budapest*, and the briefcase device is in any event so trite that one cannot imagine anyone's being eager to claim authorship of it. Nevertheless, RKO had bought the Hungarian property and, as far as the legal department was concerned, it was part of *Top Hat*. In those days before the adoption of stringent writer-producer agreements, studios were frequently sued for (and frequently guilty of) plagiarism. RKO didn't consider it necessary to acknowledge *A Scandal in Budapest* in its main credits on the film, but to ward off any threat of a suit, it did list it on its credit certificates. Credit certificates normally carry the names of all writers who contributed to the script, and latter-day researchers, in attempting to set the *Top Hat* record straight, have only confused it. One of the failures of modern film scholarship is its aggrandizement of *known* data and its almost total lack of interest in the unknown. The orchestrations of the musical numbers in *Top Hat* were by Edward Powell, a well-known Hollywood arranger, but because they were uncredited they remain anonymous, while cast lists compiled from official studio credit sheets include to this day the names of bit-players who were cut out of the release prints. The problem of anonymity will never be completely solved. Writers' credits are especially difficult to ascertain in the cases of movies that have been worked on anonymously, or in cases where directors exercised their option, as they frequently did, to edit and rewrite freely, sometimes with the help of a writer but often without, and without taking a writer's credit. *Top Hat* is an original screenplay and its authors are Dwight Taylor and Allan Scott in collaboration with Mark Sandrich. If any further source must be credited, it is *Gay Divorce*, in which the theme of mistaken identity is handled more adroitly than in *Top Hat*.

Insofar as any writer may take credit for establishing a "tone" in the early part of the Astaire–Rogers series, it is Dwight Taylor. The son of Laurette Taylor and Charles Taylor, the playwright and producer, he had been in Hollywood writing films since 1930. He was at RKO when *The Gay Divorcee* was being filmed, but he didn't work on it. He hadn't even bothered to go east when the Cole Porter version was produced because, he says, his mother had filed an opening-night pan with him, complaining of what the librettists had done to "your beautiful play." Ethel Barrymore's summation of Dwight as the apple of his mother's eye is quoted by his sister, Marguerite Courtney, in her book *Laurette*: "When he drew he was Augustus John. When he wrote verse he was François Villon. When he wrote fiction he was Guy de Maupassant." Laurette married another playwright, J. Hartley Manners, in 1912 (his wedding present to her was *Peg O' My Heart*); Dwight was ten. Noel Coward was widely thought to have caricatured the Manners theatrical ménage in *Hay Fever* in 1925, depicting Dwight as the messy young dilettante Simon Bliss. It was Coward, too, who in 1930 coined a watchword for Bohemian aristocracy with Elyot's "Let's be superficial" speech in *Private Lives*. As a writer, Taylor was no Coward, but most of the talkies he worked on in Hollywood—noble heartwrenchers like *If I Were Free*, with Irene Dunne and Clive Brook, *Long Lost Father*, with John Barrymore, and *Today We Live*, with Joan Crawford—were depressants to an essentially blithe spirit. When musicals returned, they liberated Taylor. With Sandrich and Berlin on *Top Hat* he shared, he says, "a kind of childlike excitement. The whole style of the picture can be summed up in the word inconsequentiality. When I left RKO a year later, Mark said to me, 'You will never again see so much of yourself on the screen.' "

Allan Scott, whose name appears on six of the Astaire–Rogers films, was the rewrite man. A Rhodes scholar from Massachusetts, his career began when he was hired by the Theatre Guild as a "high-grade press agent" to travel about the country and lecture on the meaning of *Mourning Becomes Electra*. With George Haight (who later produced *The Story of Vernon and Irene Castle* for RKO) he wrote a farce about a novelist on a lecture tour, called *Goodbye Again*. Starring Osgood Perkins, it ran for 200 performances in the same season as *Gay Divorce*. This brought him to the attention of Kay Brown, RKO's East Coast story editor, and he became an RKO contract writer at twenty-five. *Top Hat* was his first major assignment and the first of his many films with Mark Sandrich.

Spying in Venice on you isn't so easy to do: Blore, disguised as a gondolier, loses control of the situation.

The scripts for the Astaire–Rogers films in this rushed period leaned very heavily upon each other for ideas. While one film was in release another would be shooting, and the writers for the next film often looked back to what had worked before. As script preparations for *Top Hat* went along, more and more elements from *The Gay Divorcee* crept in, along with a trace of *Roberta*. Rogers appeared in the fashion show of *Roberta*; in *Top Hat* she's a model and Erik Rhodes is a dress designer. Rhodes makes his first appearance in Taylor's treatment of *Top Hat* as Albert, a Frenchman, but with the smash success of *The Gay Divorcee* he quickly became Alberto Beddini, fiery, feckless and malapropistic. Horton became more of a foof than a philanderer; the "passade" with Violet that he speaks about in the film had been, originally, one of many. The beach routine was dropped because it was *too* much like *The Gay Divorcee*. Another routine consisted of a brief sidewalk dance in front of the London theater by Fred Astaire and a *cockney* Negro boy. Taylor had conceived this to open the film, and it was eventually dropped, probably because Berlin wrote no music for it and the "gag" of blacks speaking with English accents had been pulled in *Flying Down to Rio*.

By early January, Taylor's rough-draft continuity was in the hands of Irving Berlin, and a month later he completed the first version of a finished script. Sandrich had meanwhile started Scott on the rewrite. Throughout the writing process Sandrich acted as editor and adviser, passing along revisions to Berman and Berlin as they came, first from Taylor and then from Scott. (Taylor and Scott never worked together.) Sandrich also inserted the new songs that had come from Berlin. On March 15, the Taylor–Scott script went to the mimeo department, and on the following day copies were out to the actors with individual, characteristically solicitous notes from Sandrich: "Dear Freddie: Please note that, as I told you, the first two sequences are not the way we will ultimately have them, and we have not yet written the scene after [the] 'Isn't This a Lovely Day' dance. The script is merely an estimating script, but I would love to hear any expressions you have on it. See you Monday." "Dear Eddie: Very happy to anticipate your being with us again. I thought I'd send you this script even though it is just a first draft, in case any ideas occurred to you. Best wishes." "Dear Eric: This will give you a general idea of the story. It is not a finished script, however, and I would appreciate any thoughts that you get for your part or for that of anyone else."

The estimating script of March 15 (i.e. the script on the basis of which footage is estimated) contained all the numbers that were to appear in the finished film plus two more: the sidewalk dance with the black boy and "Get Thee Behind Me, Satan," to be sung by Ginger Rogers in the tenth reel while Astaire goes to fetch a gondola. There was to be a reprise, at the end, of the title number, with both stars. Berlin, returning to Hollywood, had brought with him some show music to which he proposed to set words in Italian and English. This was "The Piccolino," spotted as the big production number. The plan was to have the song sung in Italian by some such well-known "Italian" singer as Raul Roulien or Tito Guizar, and then have Ginger Rogers translate it, in song, for Astaire's benefit. There would follow a big dance, for principals and chorus, which Hermes Pan would stage in the tradition of "The Carioca" and "The Continental." When Pan objected that Berlin's lyric was about a song rather than a dance ("Come to the Casino/ And hear them play the Piccolino"), Berlin suggested that the dance could be called "The Lido," and then the lyric could run "Come and do the Lido / It's very good for your libido." Even without this bit of hilarity, Berlin's lyric for "The Piccolino" is one of his funniest, a parody of the "Carioca-Continental" type of thing, and perfectly in keeping with the frankly bogus exoticism of the Venetian setting that had been designed for the film.

On January 9, 1935, fairly early in the day for *Top Hat*, Sandrich dictated a memo to Pandro Berman but never sent it. It read, in part: "As the latter part of our picture plays in and around the Lido in Italy, it has occurred to me that we may be able to get some tremendous values if we could have some authentic character scenes and backgrounds photographed in that locale." Sandrich must have started to initial this and then dropped his pen. It would be fascist Italy the cameras would be picking up, and this was hardly something of which he wanted to remind people who came to see *Top Hat*. It may then and there have occurred to him to swerve in the opposite direction and construct a Venice so remote from reality that no one would connect it with the Italy of the headlines. Actually, there was no reason why the locale had to be Venice—it could have been Cannes or Tangier or Monte Carlo—except that, once the art department got hold of the idea, it would hear of nothing else. Venice is itself a stage set, and Polglase's designers needed little prompting to get into the right spirit. The Big White Set normally occupied the largest share of the physical

costs of production. For Venice the studio decided to shoot the works. Two adjoining sound stages were flung open, a winding canal was built across both of them, and this was spanned by two staircase bridges at one end and a flat bridge at the other. It is across this latter bridge that Astaire dances Rogers in "Cheek to Cheek." "The Piccolino" takes place around the bend on the main piazza, a giant stage sheathed in red bakelite. The set was the Lido seen as one huge gleaming fairground, with dance floors, balconies, and restaurants on terraces. It was built to the second story and painted in candy-cane colors. The water was dyed black. At one point in the film, sea-planes are seen landing on the lagoon next to the hotel. This also was pure fantasy—a stock shot left over from *Flying Down to Rio*. The Venetian interiors are similarly improbable: bedrooms the size of concert halls, with satin furnishings that scream Hollywood. The designers were trying to exaggerate, trying to be artificial, and they succeeded.

Van Nest Polglase (1898–1968) did not personally design the sets in this or any other RKO picture. His name on the films is an inclusive term standing for the RKO art department. It has also come to stand for the style in décor that was this department's specialty in the Astaire–Rogers musicals. Brooklyn-born, Polglase was a student of architecture and interior decoration when he started working in movies in 1919, at the Famous Players-Lasky studio, which became Paramount. In 1932, he joined Carroll Clark at RKO and the two worked there together for eleven years, after which Polglase moved to Columbia. As head of his department at RKO, Polglase read scripts, estimated budgets and handed out assignments. He undoubtedly collaborated in an advisory capacity on designs, but the actual designing was done by draftsmen under the supervision of a unit art director. On all but one of the Astaire–Rogers films the unit art director was Carroll Clark (1894–1968). We probably should use Clark's name instead of Polglase's when we speak of the décor in these movies (the name Polglase just seems to call it all up), although no single person appears to have been responsible for it.

Taylor returned to the writing of *Top Hat* on March 11, and on April 6 produced a final script that was the sum of his and Scott's best efforts so far. Now Sandrich and Scott together worked it over once more, tightening and polishing until they had a shooting script on May 8. Meanwhile, shooting had started. Scott continued to revise on the set. Broderick's line, "All's fair in love and war and this is revolution," was given to Astaire. When Astaire helps Rogers down from the hansom cab, his line, "Don't I even get a kind word?" and her clumsy riposte, "The kindest thing I can think of at the moment is that you're hopelessly but harmlessly mad," were changed to "Don't I even get any thanks?" and "(*Tipping him*) Buy yourself a new hat." When she slaps him for the second time, saying "How could I have fallen in love with anyone as low as you?" his fadeout line was added: "She loves me." The most quoted line in the film is the motto of the House of Beddini, delivered with supreme flourish by Erik Rhodes: "For the women the kiss, for the men the sword." This was originally written, "For the men the sword, for the women the whip," and was changed when the Hays office objected. (The Hays office objected to a number of things in *Top Hat* but not, strangely, to the liaison between Rhodes and Rogers, which seems pretty free for its day.)

Shooting ended in June and the first public previews were held in July.

Top Hat *denouement. BATES: To put you off the scent I thought of many little disguises. I turned my collar around like this and very cleverly I became a clergyman. BEDDINI: You are the one that married us! BATES:*

At Santa Barbara there were some complaints about the length of the last portion of the film. ("Get Thee Behind Me, Satan" had already been deleted because it slowed down the plot; the idea of the "Italian" singer in "The Piccolino" had been discarded.) The carnival sequence was shortened and heavy cuts were made in the gondola parade that had been filmed in order to display the huge set. All other cuts concerned dialogue scenes that were inessential to continuity: various leisurely comings and goings, extraneous gag material, a few extraneous characters. In some cast lists for *Top Hat* the names of Donald Meek and Florence Roberts appear. They were to have been "a mild English curate and his faded wife" who happen along when Rhodes is threatening Horton with a fencing foil in the room above the bridal suite at the Lido hotel—because the room belongs to them. There were further cuts involving the carabinieri who are trailing Blore, who had been assigned by Horton to trail Rogers: "Calling all gondolas . . . calling all gondolas. Peeping Tomasinos along the East Canal." After a total of ten minutes was cut out, the film ran 105 minutes. When it opened at the Radio City Music Hall on August 29, it was down to 101 minutes. One of the final deletions was a scene explaining how Blore is arrested—for masquerading as a gondolier and for insulting the Italian cop who just happens to be carrying an English phrase book. (This scene exists in some prints.) *Top Hat* cost $620,000 to make, and it grossed $3 million. Next to *Mutiny on the Bounty*, it made more money than any film released in 1935.

Yes, sir. DALE: *Then we've never been really married!* BATES: *Precisely, miss.* JERRY: *Well, well, Mr. Beddini, what are you doing in this young lady's room?* (Horton, Broderick, Blore, Rogers, Astaire, Rhodes.)

"Let's Face the Music and Dance"–Scene One. With bit players Jane Hamilton, Lucille Ball, Maxine Jennings and Lita Chevret.

Follow the Fleet

An RKO Radio Picture released February 20, 1936

Producer **Pandro S. Berman** Director **Mark Sandrich** Screenplay **Dwight Taylor** and **Allan Scott,** founded on the play *Shore Leave* by **Hubert Osborne,** as produced by **David Belasco** Music and Lyrics **Irving Berlin** Musical Direction **Max Steiner** Dance Direction **Hermes Pan** Photography **David Abel** Photographic Effects **Vernon Walker** Art Director **Van Nest Polglase** Associate Art Director **Carroll Clark** Set Dressing **Darrell Silvera** Gowns **Bernard Newman** Technical Adviser **U.S.N. Lt. Cmmdr. Harvey Haislip** Music Recording **P.J. Faulkner Jr.** Recording **Hugh McDowell Jr.** Editor **Henry Berman** Sound Cutter **George Marsh** Running Time 110 minutes

Songs: "We Saw the Sea," "Let Yourself Go," "Get Thee Behind Me, Satan," "I'd Rather Lead a Band," "But Where Are You?" "I'm Putting All My Eggs in One Basket," "Let's Face the Music and Dance"

Fred Astaire *Bake Baker* **Ginger Rogers** *Sherry Martin* **Randolph Scott** *Bilge Smith* **Harriet Hilliard** *Connie Martin* **Astrid Allwyn** *Iris Manning* **Harry Beresford** *Capt. Ezra Hickey* **Russell Hicks** *Nolan* **Brooks Benedict** *Sullivan* **Ray Mayer** *Dopey* **Lucille Ball** *Kitty* **Betty Grable, Joy Hodges, Jeanne Gray, Addison Richards, Edward Burns, Frank Mills, Frank Jenks**

"We Saw the Sea." With Randolph Scott and chorus.

The Film. One way to keep star vehicles moving is to put them into reverse. *Follow the Fleet* banished continental chic by casting Astaire as a gum-chewing sailor and Rogers as a dance-hall hostess in a setting of San Francisco harbor lights, dime-a-dance palaces and apartments with sad little kitchens. The battleship in the film is stark white, and the big romantic duet, to "Let's Face the Music and Dance," surpasses all the previous ones in glamor—it's the whole fantasy of continental chic concentrated in one number; but for the most part, the atmosphere of the film is about as elegant as glazed chintz. *The Gay Divorcee, Roberta* and *Top Hat* were all evocations of the past. *Follow the Fleet* takes a flying leap into the mid-Thirties, the era of swing. It was modern rather than *moderne,* and it was the big change everybody was ready for. Although it contains some of the all-time best Astaire–Rogers numbers, it is seldom revived today. We've lost the point of its novelty, and its plot—which was certainly not novel—is a dead weight.

The ostensible source of the screenplay, the 1922 play *Shore Leave,* had also been the basis of the Youmans musical *Hit the Deck,* which RKO filmed in 1930. And either *Shore Leave* or *Hit the Deck* is the basis of practically every musical about sailors that has been made since. The plot concerned two sailors—one comic and one straight—named Smith; Bilge, the hero, spurns the heroine out of pride when she inherits a fortune and buys him a ship. *Follow the Fleet* uses the boy, the girl and the ship in the Randolph Scott–Harriet Hilliard plot. Astaire's role was suggested by Bat Smith, the comic relief, and Rogers' character probably owes something to the dance-hall hostess played by Clara Bow in the *The Fleet's In!* in 1928. Apart from these elements, though, *Follow the Fleet* is *Roberta* all over again. The dual-romance structure of that film is slavishly copied, with Astaire and Rogers spending most of their time trying to help

82

her drab of a sister, Hilliard, hook his Navy buddy, Scott, and with Astrid Allwyn taking Claire Dodd's role as the rich bitch who pursues Scott only to be foiled by Astaire. As in *Roberta*, Fred has a band—it seems that he took it over from Gene Raymond in *Flying Down to Rio*—and, as in both those films, Ginger does a number as a band vocalist. At the end of all three movies, Fred, Ginger and the band give a show in aid of a worthy cause—in *Follow the Fleet* it's to pay off her sister's debts. *Roberta* came as close to plotlessness as that ideal Astaire-Rogers musical we all like to think they should have made, but this was presumably unintentional. *Follow the Fleet* filled *Roberta*'s vacuities with plot; it wrote out all the clichés instead of leaving us to guess at them. When Irene Dunne unaccountably softened her makeup and emerged as a princess in *Roberta*, it was some sort of event, but when mousy little Miss Hilliard undergoes a similar kind of transformation, it's one of those "take-off-your-glasses,-why-you're-beautiful" things.

Coming along at the rate of two a year, the films posed a problem for the writers which they solved in the simplest way—by falling back on the last script but one. Thus *Top Hat* reworks *The Gay Divorcee* and *Follow the Fleet* reworks *Roberta*, which reworked *Flying Down to Rio*. There was just enough variation in the material to make the successive reworkings seem new, and audiences probably enjoyed seeing the new forms in which the alternating plots appeared. Astaire and Rogers were just as charming when they played old friends wise to each other's ways as when the script has them meeting for the first time. Here they are former vaudeville partners who are reunited when the fleet piles into the dance hall where she works. He's a bit callous and she's the sentimental one—another reversal. Very appropriately, the signature of the old act is the "Bugle Call Rag" fanfare last heard in the dance to "I'll Be Hard to Handle." (It was an old hoofers' cue—one blast and a flashy dance break automatically followed; Astaire used it several times in his films.) The only advantage of the *Rio-Roberta-Fleet* script over the *Divorcee-Top Hat-Swing Time* script was that it possessed a ready-made song-and-dance plot. The writers didn't have to work as hard to fit the numbers into the action. No effort at all was made to work "Let's Face the Music and Dance" into the plot; it's a completely self-contained number that creates its own drama. It is also unique, uncharacteristic of the Astaire-Rogers series.

The characteristic Astaire–Rogers romantic duet extends the love story or displaces it entirely in a stylized erotic fantasy. When the plot doesn't support

83

Harriet Hilliard meets an expert on sailors: Lucille Ball.

the fantasy by opening up a situation for it, the whole movie seems wrong. In *Follow the Fleet* the trouble isn't so much the two-young-couples formula (though it was never used again) or even that other couple (though Randolph Scott and Harriet Hilliard go together like red whiskey and Seconal) as it is the inability of the writers to break the Astaire-Rogers characters out of the comic-relief mold in time for the big dance. They did make one gruelling attempt in the scene of Rogers' audition (to the reprise of "Let Yourself Go"), and the film nearly collapses; it turns sour and begins to plod. I wish Berman and Sandrich had let Rogers double the roles of the sisters, so that there could have been one "straight" and one funny Ginger tying the two stories together. Sandrich and Allan Scott did try it years later at Paramount, when they cast Betty Hutton in a dual role in *Here Come the Waves*, yet another Navy musical.

By 1936 Rogers' position was that of co-star going on star. One reason the numbers in *Follow the Fleet* are as great as they are is that Rogers had improved so remarkably as a dancer. Under Astaire's coaching she had developed extraordinary range, and the numbers in the film are designed to show it off, from the terrific unhinged gaiety and force of "Let Yourself Go" to the zany comedy of "I'm Putting All My Eggs in One Basket" to the limpid grandeur of "Let's Face the Music and Dance." The haunting possibilities of two Gingers in the story portion of the film are strongly implied in the very ranginess of the numbers. Imagine "Eggs" the shambles of a rehearsal it is—but with the straight Ginger trying to get the hang of an unfamiliar routine. Imagine "Let's Face the Music" with this same Ginger and with Fred switching to her as his true love at the end of the film. . . . Instead of isolated feats of virtuosity, we might have had a sense-making story to match the brilliant sense of the dances. And for Rogers, instead of a return to the waitress-manicurist-chorine roles of her early movie days, we might have had the kind of dance characterization that had been written into Astaire's role in *Top Hat*. But at RKO there was neither the time nor the inclination to disrupt the conventional formulas that brought success. With all its flaws *Follow the Fleet* was a shattering hit.

"Let Yourself Go."With Joy Hodges, Betty Grable and Jeanne Gray.

The Numbers. "We Saw the Sea" is a military march with an *H.M.S. Pinafore* sort of lyric, sung at the start of the movie by Astaire on board a battleship and reprised minutes later with the male chorus as the crew starts for San Francisco on shore leave. It is not a dance number, but there are a few acrobatic tosses executed by Astaire with the men.

"Let Yourself Go." Sung by Ginger Rogers with a trio consisting of Betty Grable, Joy Hodges and Jeanne Gray, and danced to by Rogers and Astaire as the winning entry in the Paradise Ballroom dance contest. Here in a capsule are the swinging Thirties, the era of Benny Goodman and "Stompin' at the Savoy." Some of the best exhibition dancing was done in the dance halls of that period by nonprofessionals, and for this sequence Hermes Pan recruited a group of them from the Palomar and from other ballrooms around Los Angeles. In the cutting room, Astaire and Rogers, whose routine was filmed separately, were pitted against the snazziest of these couples. Astaire's choreography is a sharp, funny commentary on the eccentricities of the Lindy; he plays with the style but he doesn't imitate the steps, and for the purposes of the dance his is the one true and inimitable style. The stars "take" the competition, in this most genuine-looking of rigged movie contests, by becoming more and more coolly sensational, then pouncing like wildcats. Although they seldom do stunts, there is one beautifully, arrogantly controlled lift at the beginning of this dance; and if there is one killer step, I think it's the one that is quoted in the second flip sequence of this book. Just look at those crazy legs! Yet it's only one pow effect among dozens. On this kind of form, these two are like brilliant comedians who crack superb jokes without waiting for the laughs. Notice, too, how Astaire uses his arms and hands quite a lot while Rogers hardly uses hers at all, and how each way seems to lend its own comic emphasis to the big, tough jazz step that this is.

"Get Thee Behind Me, Satan" and "But Where Are You?" are sung by Harriet Hilliard in two solo spots that are always cut on television. The first is a soliloquy inserted between the vocal and the dance to "Let Yourself Go"; the

Above and facing page: "I'd Rather Lead a Band." The sailor on the saxophone is Tony Martin.

second takes place at a party and is another soliloquy since none of the guests pay poor Miss Hilliard the least attention. She was a radio vocalist with Ozzie Nelson's orchestra and this was her first film. A blonde, she turned brunette for the film out of deference to Ginger Rogers.

"I'd Rather Lead a Band." Astaire's gift for dramatization is most purely expressed in his singles. With the possible exception of "I Won't Dance" in *Roberta*, they were never straight technical exhibitions. He could make a story out of the dynamic variety of tap dancing. With him, a dance impulse and a dramatic motive seem to be indivisible and spontaneous, so that we get that little kick of imaginative sympathy every time he changes the rhythm or the speed or the pressure of a step. And though we don't perceive the dance as "drama," the undertone of motivation continually sharpens and refreshes our interest in what we do see, rather like an attractive mannerism in speech.

It takes a master to fascinate in this way, but Astaire doesn't stop here. He presents a second and different kind of story. Sailors emerge in lines and he drills them, tapping out his commands. He "reviews the troops." Then,

as they march in place, setting up a base rhythm, he is galvanized by the beat. Mark time changes to double time, the men jog off and he's alone for a smashing pure-dance finale. Curiously, he didn't make the number out of the idea of leading a band—he saved that for *Second Chorus* (1940). Nor does the success of the number depend on the drill-routine idea—it's just another way of producing himself, an extension of a dramatic instinct that is on view at all times. I imagine that this instinct, or skill, was exciting on the stage; in movies, at short range and within a concentrated field of focus, it is phenomenal. Astaire possessed the secret of the paradox: he possessed perpetual spontaneity on film.

"Let Yourself Go" reprise. Ginger Rogers auditions for a theatrical producer. She dances, but when she tries to sing, she can't bring out the notes because Fred, thinking he's doing her a good turn, has put bicarbonate of soda in her drinking water. The scene is very carefully not played for laughs. The mini-crisis that ensues in the relatively carefree Fred-Ginger story is supposed to take our minds off the fact that Astaire and Rogers are really playing second leads, but the manufactured complications don't suggest a serious turn of events; they suggest comedy misplayed.

This sick little episode is worth suffering through for Rogers' tap solo. It's easy to underrate Rogers' dancing because she never appeared to be working

hard, and because, with a bold nonchalance that irritates women more than it does men, she sometimes threw away stuff she never had. But Rogers danced with love, with pride in the beauty of an illusion—and with one of the most elegant dancer's bodies imaginable. She avoided any suggestion of toil or inadequacy. She was physically incapable of ugliness. And how splendid and perky she looks in this number. How outrageous that the liquid hips and the strong knees should be more interesting than the tapping feet (which are over-dubbed). Choreographed by Hermes Pan, it is one of the two solos that she performs in the series. (The other is the "Yama Yama Man" in *The Castles*.)

"I'm Putting All My Eggs in One Basket." Perhaps the prize goofball routine of all time and the only one the team ever did, full of gratifying bits of nonsense that now and then seem related to their dance style—like his pulling her toward him so that she turns right into a spill—but more often aren't. Hermes Pan: "We kept on gagging it up. I remember we decided there would be a thing where she got stuck and couldn't get out of the step, which is an old burlesque gag. It was every old vaudeville trick in the world stuck into one number." It is prefaced by Fred at the piano, playing the song barrelhouse style; he then sings it with Ginger.

"Let's Face the Music and Dance." It could be subtitled "A Playlet." Astaire at the gambling tables in Monte Carlo has just lost all his money. The curtains close and reopen on the terrace at the top of the casino. He is elaborately shunned by society. Alone, he takes out a small pistol, but just then Rogers appears at the far side of the stage, twisting a long chiffon handkerchief and gazing out over the parapet. She steps up on it but he prevents the leap. Ruefully he shows her his empty wallet and the gun which she looks at unseeingly, then tries to snatch. He throws both away and *sings*.

How they get through all this without a laugh is their secret. The song is like one of those brave ballads of the Depression written by Arthur Schwartz and Howard Dietz—"Dancing in the Dark" or "Alone Together"—and the mood is awesomely grave. The dance is one of their simplest and most daring, the steps mostly walking steps done with a slight retard. The withheld impetus makes the dance look dragged by destiny, all the quick little circling steps pulled as if on a single thread. A beautiful moment occurs when he promenades her as she holds a pose on half-toe with one lifted knee. Another when they circle the stage, turning first one shoulder then the other toward each other; and when she continues the tiny steps in a series of *chaîné* turns, her hands uplifted,

and he follows with his arms encircling her waist. Still another: they turn away from each other in a swift kneel and as swiftly rise with a light jump, only to sink again on the other knee. Her dress, made of metallic threads and with weights in the sleeves and hem, winds and unwinds, a part of the dance. The exit, unforgettable, is another knee-sink but now side by side. Slowly they rise together and back off in a long *fondu*. Then: one, two, three, four paces, and they go off in a Jooss-type lunge, backs arched, one knee yanked high. At the suddenness and hugeness of it the audience does laugh, then immediately applauds its audacity.

What I find most moving in this noble and almost absurdly glamorous dance is the absence of self-enchantment in the performance. Astaire and Rogers yield nothing to Garbo's throat or Pavlova's Swan as icons of the sublime, yet their manner is brisk. *Briskly* they immolate themselves. And within the enclosed theatrical setting of the number, everything finds its place. The gesture of abandon with which Rogers tosses away her scarf at the start of the dance is also the way such a prop would be gotten rid of on the stage. Astaire did two dance dramas, "This Heart of Mine" and "Limehouse Blues," in the MGM revue *Ziegfeld Follies* (1946), but they weren't as nakedly theatrical or as powerful.

Production. Astaire's practice was to prepare and, if possible, film all but the most complicated of the dances before main production got under way. For *Follow the Fleet* he had four numbers to prepare—five, if you count the brief acrobatic routine with the men in "We Saw the Sea." Although main shooting on the film was not scheduled to begin until November 1, 1935, Astaire was at the studio and rehearsing on September 5.

By agreement with RKO, Astaire always worked in seclusion. No one was allowed in at his rehearsals except Hermes Pan, the pianist Hal Borne, and, when Astaire and Pan were ready for her, Ginger Rogers. Neither Pandro Berman nor Mark Sandrich ever saw a routine until it was pretty well set. Pan would keep them informed on the things they needed to know, such as the length of each number and the amount of extra personnel (audiences, crowds, ensemble dancers, dummy orchestras) that would be involved. Generally, though, these considerations would be determined in advance. Astaire always knew how much space he would have on the set and how much time in the script.

He knew, too, what story points went with what dances, even though a final shooting script would not be available until after production had started

and even though the score might not yet have been completed. In *Follow the Fleet* Astaire knew that there would be a dance contest which he and Rogers would enter, and that later there would be a slapstick rehearsal number for them both. The dance contest was evidently cooked up in story conferences before the writing began; in Dwight Taylor's first script it is well established (although the Berlin number that Taylor had spotted at that point was not "Let Yourself Go" but "Moonlight Maneuvers"). The slapstick routine, however, appears to have originated in that same script, which Astaire had when he went into rehearsal. Taylor had "Bat and Ginger" practicing on the ship, and his directions were that "during this impromptu dancing they continue to insult each other, somewhat like the old dance teams in the 'Two-a-day.'" There followed dialogue, over which Sandrich wrote in flaming red pencil: "Situation! NUMBER." It did become a number, evolved in rehearsal, but with pantomime instead of patter.

Berlin might have written "I'm Putting All My Eggs in One Basket" for this number after it was developed, or he might have pulled it out of his trunk. It's an appropriately corny pop tune with a slight rural flavor (the yodeling notes on "I'm betting ev'rything I've got on you") that does suggest some ancient vaudeville turn, but it was of no great importance to the dance. In fact, the dance just kicks it around, and one feels that almost any song would have filled the purpose. There is no such feeling about "Let Yourself Go." This song must have been intended for the dance that was set to it (the spaced imitative phrases of the verse just *sound* like a contest), and one reason it's incorrectly spotted in Taylor's first script is that it hadn't yet been completed. Astaire had a great deal of freedom in his choice and use of material, and with every film he tried to do something new. What he obviously wanted here was a big hot swinging number that was as close as possible to the sound of the big dance bands that were then making news across the country. He was on excellent terms with Irving Berlin and undoubtedly knew more about the character of the songs that Berlin was writing than the scriptwriters did.

Except for the writing of the songs, Astaire controlled every phase of the development of a number, and there are probably numerous instances in which he even affected the actual composing. The songs did not pass through an arranger before they came to him. They came to him directly, and the arrangement was laid out, after weeks of rehearsal, at Hal Borne's piano. Astaire is himself a trained musician and he knew how to manipulate a composition for

maximum theatrical effect without distortion. Composers trusted him. Berlin has said that he would rather have Astaire introduce his songs than any other performer, and Kern, a notably fussy man who concerned himself with every aspect of production, used to say, "Astaire *can't* do anything bad."

Astaire chose his assistants, Hermes Pan and Hal Borne, at the start of his movie career, on *Flying Down to Rio.* Hermes Pan (born Hermes Panagiotopulos in Memphis, Tennessee) had no formal dance training. After singing in *Top Speed*, he made his way to Hollywood where he was hired as a dancer in Grauman's Chinese Theater prologues by LeRoy Prinz, who had been one of the dance directors on *Top Speed.* Pan then picked up more experience performing and putting on dances in a tab show that toured the West Coast. He was working as a dancer and assistant stage manager in a Hollywood revue when he tried out as Dave Gould's assistant. Gould assigned him to the Astaire–Rogers portion of "The Carioca," and from then on he was Astaire's assistant. He was also responsible for the ensemble dances in the Astaire films, and, as dance director of RKO, for the dances in other films. Pan looks a great deal like Astaire, dances like him, and even talks like him, but until "The Carioca" he had not met him, nor had he ever seen Astaire on the stage. As a mirror image, illuminating Astaire's conceptions and contributing ideas that he could use, Pan has been more helpful to Astaire than any other choreographer. Together they have made nineteen films and four television specials.

Hal Borne is today a prominent Hollywood-Las Vegas composer, arranger and conductor best known for the acts he has built for such entertainers as Sammy Davis, Dean Martin, Tony Martin and Cyd Charisse. The only credit he ever received on an Astaire picture was on *Second Chorus*, as the composer of "I Ain't Hep to That Step But I'll Dig It." A classically trained pianist, he moved with his family from Chicago to Los Angeles in 1933 and was hired by Max Steiner, the RKO musical director, to be the studio's recording pianist. As a newcomer, Borne wasn't allowed by the musicians' local to record right away, so he waited out his time doing "sideline"—playing the piano in the dummy orchestras that were filmed (but not recorded). He was twenty-one years old, a few years younger than Hermes Pan, and had a gift for jazz improvisation. During a break one day on the "Orchids in the Moonlight" set, Astaire, who was looking for a rehearsal pianist, heard Borne playing and told Steiner, "I think we've got a piano."

A well-known photograph of Astaire and Pan in rehearsal shows Astaire

Below and following pages: "Let's Face the Music and Dance"—Scene Two.

in a dance pose while Pan points to a blackboard covered with incomprehensible markings. The photograph was staged for publicity and bears no relation to what went on in rehearsal. There were no boards, no diagrams, no notation. Astaire and Pan would begin by listening as Hal Borne played. Then they would start moving about, experimenting with different approaches, taking the music in small sections. Astaire's numbers were generally conceived within a format. Solos and tap duets often started in an easy rhythm and then exploded into double and triple time. In the solos there was usually a section without music which Astaire would fill with pure dance invention to a metronomic or figured base laid down by Borne, or sometimes there would be an interlude of pantomime. ("I'd Rather Lead a Band" contains both ideas.) The romantic duets would begin with a slow *legato* section, perhaps include a *staccato* repeat for a bit of soft shoe before building to a stormy climax (usually to the music of the release) and then subside or rise once more in the final moments. Like the dance band arrangers of the day, Astaire used a strong beat in a ballad, and he choreographed to the accompaniment as well as to the melody. It was an ingenious, tricky style to master because it did not mimic the music. Astaire preferred sequences that ran alongside the music in unpredictable phrase-patterns or against it in a countercurrent. And it was difficult, too, because he had a horror of repeating himself and was always looking for new steps and for new ideas for routines. Sometimes the new steps or ideas would be suggested by a song or a lyric, sometimes by a script situation and sometimes they would be worked out, so to speak, in the abstract. Borne would improvise, building extended figures around the written notes, or making up dummy tunes if the songs weren't ready. Astaire would pick up on this, and Borne in turn would pick up on Astaire's and Pan's movements as they danced. Work would continue in this improvisatory fashion until Astaire was satisfied. If the number

was a duet, Pan would assume Rogers' role and would teach it to her and rehearse her before she rehearsed with Astaire. "With Fred I'd be Ginger," he says, "and with Ginger I'd be Fred."

"Moonlight Maneuvers" and "There's a Smile on My Face," both published in 1935, were two Berlin songs discarded from *Follow the Fleet* before filming. Sandrich tried hard to get the former, a tinkling tune about sailors meeting their girls, into the film, and in one of the early scripts it is a production number for Rogers and the chorus in the show that is staged at the end of the film. In this show "Let's Face the Music and Dance" was to have been sung by Connie when RKO was hoping to lure Irene Dunne into playing the part. "There's a Smile on My Face," also a number for Connie, dropped out when "Get Thee Behind Me, Satan" was transferred from *Top Hat*.

As soon as he had a shooting script, Sandrich went through it with a stopwatch. A minute-by-minute analysis of the whole production was prepared in the form of a big multicolored chart. Each scene was broken down into its components, and their proportions in terms of time were represented in bar-lengths of different colors: blue for music (accompaniment and underscoring), green for singing, red for dancing, yellow for novelty (e.g. the dance lesson that Astaire gives the sailors in *Fleet*), white for story (action and dialogue), orange for inserts, black for optical effects. The charts were prepared at the request of studio efficiency experts who wanted to keep down costs by avoiding cutting-room-floor spillage, but they were also useful to Sandrich in planning the distribution of numbers and timing these in relation to the plot. He prepared a detailed minutage for every musical he made. (A portion of the one for *Follow the Fleet* appears on pages 186–187).

Sandrich's triumphs as a director were in the sequences that dovetailed the musical numbers and the story: "The Continental," "No Strings," the title number of *Shall We Dance*. His best work in *Follow the Fleet* is the Paradise Ballroom sequence, mixing two songs, two plots and a dance. But what his charts didn't show and didn't plan for is the disparity in quality between the numbers and the story. We tumble from peaks into shallows. Sandrich's estimated running time for *Follow the Fleet* was 97 minutes, with the numbers accounting for 28 of those minutes. It is not a bad ratio, and the thirteen additional minutes that were shot didn't change it by adding anything to the script. Incredibly, the ratio is the same in *Roberta*, which seems all numbers. Where *Roberta* is ineffable, *Fleet* is a bore. What a difference a plot makes.

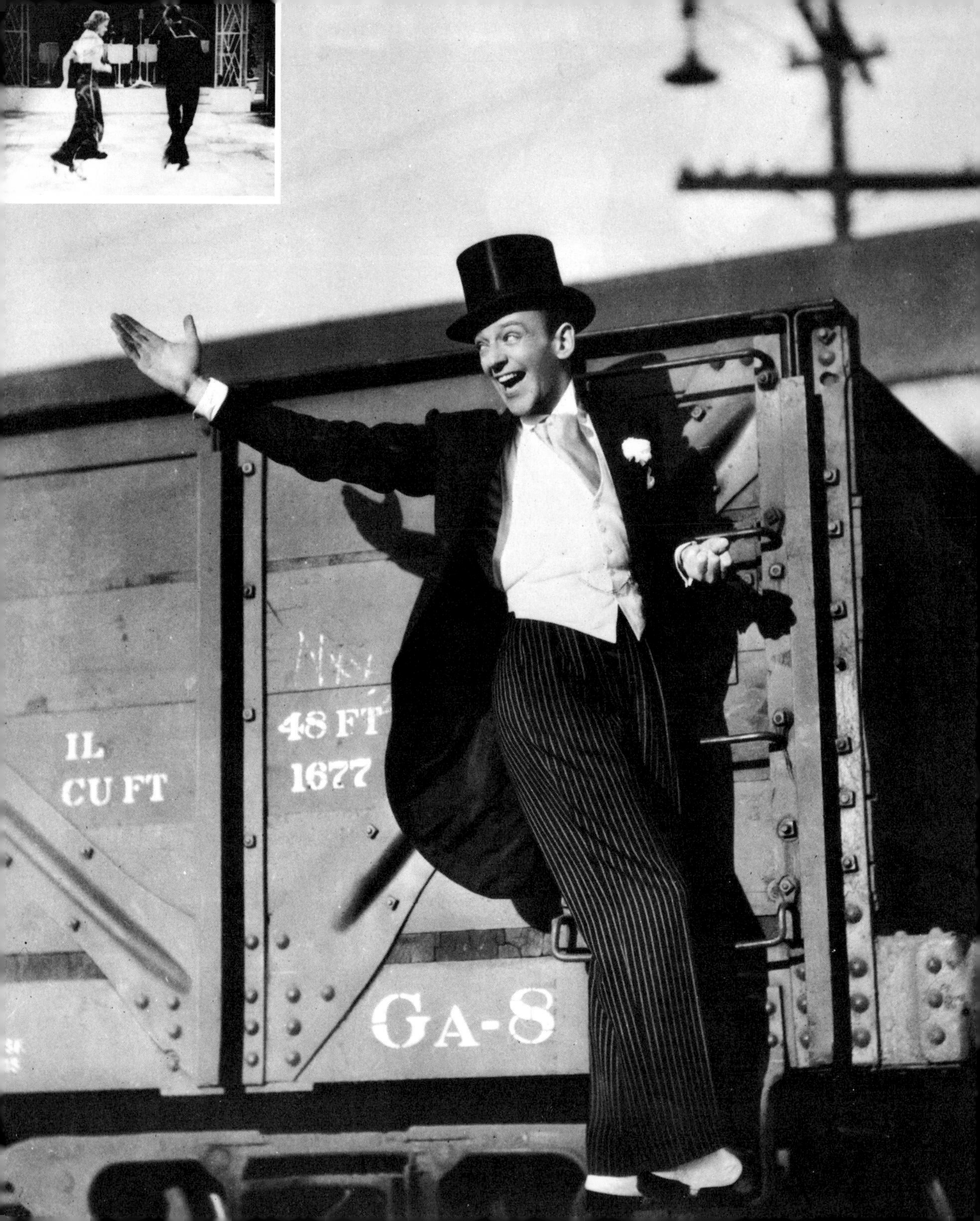
IL
CU FT
48 FT
1677
GA-8

Swing Time

An RKO Radio Picture released September 4, 1936

Producer **Pandro S. Berman** Director **George Stevens** Screenplay **Howard Lindsay** and **Allan Scott,** based on a story by **Erwin Gelsey** Music by **Jerome Kern** Lyrics by **Dorothy Fields** Musical Direction **Nathaniel Shilkret** Dance Ensembles Staged by **Hermes Pan** Photography **David Abel** Photographic Effects **Vernon Walker** Art Director **Van Nest Polglase** Associate Art Director **Carroll Clark** Silver Sandal set and "Bojangles" costumes designed by **John Harkrider** Set Dressing **Darrell Silvera** Gowns **Bernard Newman** Recording **Hugh McDowell Jr.** Editor **Henry Berman** Sound Cutter **George Marsh** Running Time 105 minutes

Songs: "Pick Yourself Up," "The Way You Look Tonight," "Waltz in Swing Time," "A Fine Romance," "Bojangles of Harlem," "Never Gonna Dance"

Fred Astaire *John Garnett ("Lucky")* **Ginger Rogers** *Penny Carrol* **Victor Moore** *Dr. Cardetti ("Pop")* **Helen Broderick** *Mabel* **Eric Blore** *Mr. Gordon* **Georges Metaxa** *Ricardo Romero* **Betty Furness** *Margaret Watson* **Landers Stevens** *Judge Watson* **John Harrington** *Raymond* **Pierre Watkin** *Simpson* **Abe Reynolds** *Tailor* **Gerald Hamer** *Eric Facannistrom* **Edgar Dearing** *Policeman* **Harry Bernard** *Stage Hand* **Ralph Byrd** *Hotel Clerk* **Charles Hall** *Chauffeur* **Jean Perry** *Roulette Dealer* **Olin Francis** *Muggsy* **Floyd Shackleford** *Butler* **Fern Emmett** *Maid* **Howard Hickman** *First Minister* **Ferdinand Munier** *2nd Minister* **Joey Ray** *Announcer* **Frank Jenks, Jack Goode, Donald Kerr, Ted O'Shea, Frank Edmunds, Bill Brand** *Dancers*

Below: "Pick Yourself Up." Right: Arranging for a dance lesson ("To know how to dance is to know how to control oneself"). Fred fatuous, Blore obliging, Ginger raging within.

The Film. *Swing Time* is a movie about a myth, the myth of Fred and Ginger and the imaginary world of romance they live in. It is a world of nighttime frolics very much like *Top Hat*'s, but it is also a middle-class, workaday, American world. It is top hats and empty pockets: Fred as a Depression dandy hopping a freight car, Ginger being sung to with soap in her hair. The antithetical strain runs through the picture, and, stilted and unsure of its effects as *Swing Time* often is, its conceits are so graceful, so alive to the mythical power of its subject, that it seems to me the true miracle film of the series, the one that as a follow-up to the unfollowable *Top Hat* shouldn't have worked but did. *Swing Time* is based on *Top Hat*, not as a remake, but as a jazz rhapsody might be based on a classic theme; its materials are romantic irony, contrast, the fantasy of things going in reverse. The snow of *Swing Time* is as magical as the rain of "Isn't This a Lovely Day?" and the white hotels of Venice. If you put *Top Hat* in a glass ball like a paperweight and turned it upside down, it would be *Swing Time*. And at the end of *Swing Time*, the sun comes out through the falling snow.

It was first announced under the title *I Won't Dance*, after Astaire's hit song in *Roberta*. This was changed to *Never Gonna Dance*, and negation persisted as the motif of the film. *Follow the Fleet* contradicted the Fred and Ginger myth by deglamorizing the stars. *Swing Time* put back the glamor, but the duets were written and staged contrariwise, with a provocativeness derived in part from shrewd show-business switch-hitting and in part from genuine ironic wit. In "Pick Yourself Up" Fred pretends he can't dance so that he can be taught by Ginger. "The Way You Look Tonight" is deliberately anti-romantic (although Ginger with her shampoo coiffure is about as unattractive as Fred is clumsy in "Pick Yourself Up"). "A Fine Romance" is subtitled "A Sarcastic Love Song." The twist in "Never Gonna Dance" is that the climactic duet of the film is a dance of parting, its mood one of frustration and defeat.

The game of piquet: Rogers with Helen Broderick, Astaire with Gerald Hamer and Victor Moore.

In the other Astaire–Rogers films we sat around waiting for them to dance. In *Swing Time* the agony of waiting is part of the plot. After "Pick Yourself Up" the whole movie is taken up with trying to get to the "Waltz in Swing Time." When finally we come to the night of the Waltz, fresh blows start falling: "There isn't going to be any dance . . . any music . . . any dance." The owner of the Silver Sandal Café has lost the orchestra to the Mafia-run Club Raymond. Fred wins it back at Raymond's roulette table, but the orchestra leader, in love with Ginger and jealous of Fred, refuses to play. Fred flings up the leader's baton arm and starts the music with a crash. (Since they'd been engaged by the Silver Sandal, it makes no sense for Fred and Ginger to be doing their Waltz at Raymond's, but they can't wait another second and neither can we.) Later on, we arrive at the same impasse when the mob wins the orchestra back from Fred: "There isn't going to be any dance."

Though there are discontinuities in the plot, *Swing Time* is faithful to its myth. In the last reversal of the film, the line changes to "There isn't going to be any wedding" when Ginger is about to marry the nasty bandleader, Georges Metaxa. The tables are turned at last, frustration is dissolved and the whole scene is played with the entire cast falling about the set in fits of laughter. The suggestive dance-marriage rhyme is one of the most wonderful things that ever happened in an Astaire–Rogers movie, but contagious-laughter scenes run terrible risks—they're usually ice-cold—and George Stevens seems to have set out to stage the biggest laughing jag since Laurel and Hardy's in *Leave 'Em Laughing* (on which he had worked as the cameraman). In a way, he was right to attempt it. "There isn't going to be any wedding" is a sweet payoff to the running "gag" of the film, but it's basically intellectual comedy, a concept alien to American movies. Stevens wanted the boffo ending, only he didn't have enough gag material to set it up. Two years later he made the same mistake

"The Way You Look Tonight."

in the all-crying finale of *Vivacious Lady,* again a contagion gag but with even less plot justification than the laughter of *Swing Time.* The writers of *Swing Time* had arranged a symmetrical plot that ended, as it had begun, with a wedding (a misalliance) not taking place. When Fred thinks he has to marry Betty Furness (a nondancer), Victor Moore steals his trousers. When Ginger thinks she has to marry Metaxa (a nondancer and a pill), Fred steals Metaxa's. All Stevens had was this one tedious prep-school prank. So he gunned the engines and bulled through. There's no reason for Helen Broderick to be laughing as hard as she is when she doesn't yet know that the wedding won't occur. Stevens begs laughs all over the place, especially at the expense of poor Metaxa without his pants. But on the crest of the laughter he rises to one of the pinnacles of American romantic comedy. A bewildered clergyman asks, "What about the wedding?" and Ginger, light breaking through at last, repeats the now reverberant line *"There isn't going to be any wedding!"* At that moment the beauty of it hits her, and she, too, collapses in laughter. "One of the virtues of having a system of values," said Virginia Woolf, "is that you know exactly what to laugh at." In a dance film the dance values are more lucid and exciting to the mind than any other kind. In *Swing Time* they grip with the logic of a metaphor: the dance as love, the lovers as dancers. And the dancers as stars. There never was a more star-struck movie or a greater dance musical.

Like *Top Hat,* it is full of nostalgia for the high life of the Twenties, for what Stanley Walker called "the night club era." Manhattan is glamorized as a town where fortunes are openly made and lost each night at the roulette tables, a slight breach of history. The film freely mixes Twenties and Thirties references: Rogers calls an unfriendly policeman a "Cossack," and, later, Astaire and Victor Moore picket her with signs, like Ford workers. But "Eric Facannistrom," the lush who demolishes Astaire at the game of piquet, is a character

out of the Wodehousian world of *Top Hat* and *The Gay Divorcee*. The dancing school where Ginger Rogers works is pure Thirties; in 1936 the Arthur Murray studios were at a peak of popularity, and it's not fanciful to suppose that the Astaire–Rogers movies had something to do with this. (Astaire himself later opened a chain of studios.)

A cycle in the series closes with *Swing Time*. Up to this point, the vehicles fashioned for Astaire and Rogers had cannibalized each other for ideas. With *Shall We Dance* they began appropriating ideas from other contemporary Hollywood films. A certain family tone is lost, and the team almost seems to be seeking its own dissolution. *Swing Time* is an apotheosis. No more changes were left to be rung on the mythical theme of Fred and Ginger. Astaire and Rogers had set trends. Now, on the momentum of their style, they would follow them to the end of the decade.

The Numbers. The songs are more tightly interwoven with the script—and with each other—than in any of the other Astaire–Rogers films. For *Swing Time*, Jerome Kern and Dorothy Fields wrote a real "book" musical, and I think it can be argued that it was Kern's most successful one since *Show Boat*. The ballads fit together like sprays in an exquisitely assembled bouquet, not only melodically, like "A Fine Romance" and "The Way You Look Tonight" which can be sung in counterpoint and are sung that way in the *finaletto*, but in the lyrics. Dramatically, too, the songs establish the scheme of the film, from the very first number:

"Pick Yourself Up." What is this but a piece of advice on winning through over frustration? ("Pick yourself up, dust yourself off, and start all over again.") And such is Astaire's integrity as a choreographer that the step Rogers is struggling to teach him in this scene—"three steps to the left, three steps to the right, and turn"—is the opening step of the dazzling routine they do. Unlike the other hot-rhythm duets, which go through two or three changes of speed, "Pick Yourself Up" is all in one tempo, and its compressed energy seems to ignite the air it moves in. So much happens in the coda alone, which is launched with a running leap over invisible footstools (the leap looks adorably silly) and continues in a fine madness as they lift each other back and forth over the low railing that rings the dance floor. Meanwhile, the music has switched to a new riding tune that creates a wave of exhilaration—and anxiety: they're going out but they can't possibly get out that fast. Yes, they can, and calmly: clear

With Georges Metaxa.

across to the other side and out. They walk away leaving everything in flames.

"The Way You Look Tonight." From Howard Lindsay's recollections: "I led into the song by having Ginger Rogers cooking a dinner for herself and Fred in her apartment. Her hair got into considerable disarray, and she got smudges on her forehead and cheeks. Fred started playing the song at the piano in the living room, she was drawn into the living room by the music, and when he got to the phrase 'the way you look tonight,' he glanced up and found her in this disheveled state. The producers lacked the courage to do this, so they had her washing her hair, and she entered with her hair covered with white foam, but so beautifully sculptured that it looked like a white wig." The song won the Academy Award for 1936.

"Waltz in Swing Time." Here they come again, and again the dance is all in one tempo, seemingly in one breath—a wide, white stream flowing in agile cross-rhythms, flowing without pause through so many intricacies and surprises, so many acts of mutual gallantry and faith that they can't possibly be cited, much less described. The flip pictures on these pages are a fractional glimpse of the most rapturously sustained, endlessly reseeable of all their dances. Unlike "Night and Day" or "Let's Face the Music" or "Never Gonna Dance," the Waltz has no special story to tell. It is pure white: pure vision and sound.

105

"A Fine Romance."

Nevertheless, it is one of those grand, impassioned moonlit dances, and it just flies—it's the *brio* of romance. What can one say? Two minutes and 45 seconds of unspeakable delight.

"A Fine Romance." Rogers in her caracul coat sings it to Astaire, and Astaire in his bowler sings it back. Both the song and the scene that leads up to it, with Fred blinkingly ignoring Ginger's advances (he plays it like Stan Laurel), are as knowingly and tenderly staged, directed and performed as any dance. And there's a lovely musical setting (by Edward Powell).

"Bojangles of Harlem" is the only blackface number Astaire has ever done, and even if it weren't incomparably superior to the run of such things in its day, which, in rising order of bearability, is more accurately suggested by Al Jolson in *Wonder Bar*, the "darky" number in *A Day at the Races*, and the "yassuh" butler that Floyd Shackleford plays in Astaire's own film, it would be as much worth seeing today as it was in 1936. Astaire isn't simply beyond good and evil, he's beyond good and better. The we-don't-do-these-things-anymore people should be told that we didn't do them then either, but *beyond* that, if they cared remotely for the art of dancing, they might recognize the deep dignity of homage that is in this piece—not the homage of one white to one black man, but of one great artist to another. And it is homage, not impersonation. Astaire is changeless: he isn't any more like Vernon Castle when he's doing Vernon Castle's routines than he's like Bill Robinson when he's doing one of his own and calling it "Bojangles."

"Bojangles" is in three parts, each of them more marvelous than the screen seems able to contain. Two pairs of doors slide diagonally backward to release the chorus—sepia-tinted girls, twelve in white, twelve in black. A third pair opens on Astaire reclining atop Harlem, two false legs as long as guard rails stretching toward the camera. (There's a bad moment of "amputation" when these legs are taken away.) The dance that Astaire does with the girls is as inventive a group number as any I've seen on the screen—it reminds me of Balanchine. The chorus vanishes, and a fourth pair of doors reveals a movie screen on which are flashed three Astaires in silhouette, his first use of trick photography. Here is one of those *misterioso* scenes he does so well, dancing in and out of sync with the shadows. And for a finish he taps his way toward us, tapping and clapping his hands (the white gloves have clappers in the palms) in two different rhythms that are "off" the rhythm of the music. The man who has been called the Mozart of dancers here turns Stravinskian. Just

as our senses are about to burst from the complexity of it, he wraps it up.

"Never Gonna Dance." This great plaintive ballad, incomprehensible outside the context of the film, sets the mood for the dance of dances. In the film it is the end of the affair, in life it is the end of Astaire and Rogers' Golden Age. Astaire sings of "my Penny" and of how "the wolf was discreet, he left me my feet, and so, I'll put them down on anything but the la belle, la perfectly swell, romance—never gonna dance." His monogamous instinct is to quit dancing so long as he can't dance with her. On two stage levels linked by glistening staircases there now takes place the supreme dramatic event of the series, a duet moving through a succession of darkening emotions and abrupt rhythmic changes in which we see unfolded in dance the story of the film. The dance lesson of "Pick Yourself Up" reappears as an extended reflective walk around the floor to the music of "The Way You Look Tonight." A sideways lunge face to face is the most concrete image: the hunger of blocked desire. Face to face without touching and then side by side they continue dancing. Steps from the Waltz are quoted. Finally, the two staircases flanking the stage separate them in space. And at the top of the stairs, in the fiery sweep of an exit, all ends.

Finaletto. A typical Kern ending, with the cast joining in a sweetened reprise of "A Fine Romance" (though Stevens can't make Metaxa's sudden conversion into a good sport believable), and with the stars singing in counterpoint for the first and only time. High over Manhattan the snow falls like confetti and the sun breaks out of the sky.

Production. One of the ironies of Astaire's career must be *Gay Divorce* and its aftermath. The most critical of all his shows and the one he worked the hardest to save, it became a movie that made him a star, and was the basis of his biggest movie hit *Top Hat*. When, after *Follow the Fleet*, Dwight Taylor left Hollywood to write Jessie Matthews movies in London, Pandro Berman brought in Howard Lindsay, who had directed *Gay Divorce* on Broadway.

Howard Lindsay, as he told me when I interviewed him about *Swing Time* a few years before his death in 1968, was not very experienced in the writing of screenplays. "I left Hollywood after my stint of ten or twelve weeks," he said, "and my script was completely revised by Allan Scott. He must have the credit for the picture as it stands. I tried to create for Fred Astaire and Ginger Rogers two characters whom the audience would feel belonged together.

That is how a playwright for the theater would work. When I showed this sequence to Pan Berman, he said, 'That's just a waste of footage. The minute the names of Astaire and Rogers go up on the marquee, the audience knows they belong together.' "

Lindsay's job was, as Taylor's had been, to cue in the numbers. He developed his script from the outline of a story the studio owned, about a young gambler who promises to quit the big time when he has won enough to marry the girl back home. (Was the casting of Astaire as a gambler suggested by "Let's Face the Music and Dance"?) George Stevens liked the story well enough to use a very similar one in *The Only Game in Town* (1970), but in *Swing Time* we never see how Astaire parlays Helen Broderick's ten dollars into a bankroll, and we tend to forget about the girl back home (Betty Furness). Allan Scott says he played down the gambling story, "not because I was against gambling, but because the numbers didn't come from it. They came from the love story. How Fred made all his money was supposed to be shown in a series of lap-dissolves, but we cut it all out." The only number that did come from the gambling story was the opening number, deleted before filming. It was called "It's Not in the Cards" and showed the magic act that Astaire and Moore had in vaudeville. The film opens instead on the end of the act, with Astaire dancing in front of a line of boys, but this was never a complete number and the music we hear is not the song that Kern and Fields wrote. The omission of a full number gets the movie off to a slow start, with thirty minutes elapsing before "Pick Yourself Up." (Other deletions, post-production: Astaire's journey to New York in the box car with Moore, and their arrival in the New York freight yards. When preview audiences responded stonily to the laughing scenes, they were abridged and partially reshot. Eric Blore, who never reappears in the movie, was a casualty of the retakes.)

Scott lived five blocks from Kern, and much of his work was done with Kern and Dorothy Fields at Kern's house. Miss Fields' lyrics were written to fit Kern's music. The two key songs, "Never Gonna Dance" and "A Fine Romance," were linked by the phrase "la belle romance," which was also inserted in the dialogue because, as Miss Fields says, "Kern always liked to work tidy." The systematic "negative" plotting of the numbers is credited by Scott to Kern and Fields, whom he calls "awfully show-wise people who taught me a lot."

Dorothy Fields had become Kern's lyricist on the film of *Roberta*. At the same time she continued to collaborate with Jimmy McHugh and other com-

Next page: "Bojangles of Harlem."

posers, and in 1935 she wrote the songs with McHugh for the RKO musical *Hooray for Love,* which featured Bill Robinson and Fats Waller in a Harlem sequence. Out of this came the idea for "Bojangles of Harlem." When the song arrived on Hal Borne's piano rack, it was in 2/4 time. "I played it for Fred, and he had kind of a strange look on his face," Borne recalls. "That was the trouble with Kern. His melodies were the greatest but his syncopation was corny. It was corny *then.* Fred said, 'I like the melody and the lyric is just fine, but why don't we swing it? Then we can come back to 2/4.' But it still wasn't right. And it wasn't long enough. I added a section, which I played on an upright piano. It was based on a vamp idea that kept going up different keys. That was not a harpsichord, it was a doctored piano, and that was not Kern, it was me. We always had to do these things in production numbers."

The muted, quietly flowing section of the "Waltz in Swing Time" (marked *poco meno mosso)* was added by Borne, again because there wasn't enough music. The Waltz is credited to Kern and contains glancing references to his score for the film, but it is the composition of Robert Russell Bennett, Kern's long-time arranger and orchestrator. Bennett got the assignment when Kern said to him one day, "Go and see what Freddie wants." Astaire wanted a jazz waltz, fairly extensive in form and without lyrics. The music was tailored to his specifications. Bennett, who also orchestrated the dance numbers in this film and wrote most of the background music, at first scored the Waltz for a small salon orchestra. "It was very delicate," he says, "and Freddie didn't like it. He wanted the brassy sound of a pit band. When I saw the movie, I realized he was right." Just before release, the name of the film was changed from *Never Gonna Dance* to *Swing Time,* and Dorothy Fields wrote a brief set of lyrics to be sung by a chorus over the main titles.

The two big sets in the film are both night clubs. The Silver Sandal, which is seen in two different décors, was named after the Silver Slipper on West 48th Street, one of New York's best-known night clubs. Like most of the clubs it was gone by 1932; another club with the same name was opened in the Forties. The Club Raymond was a composite of Hollywood's Clover Club, where movie people did a lot of heavy gambling, and the Rainbow Room in Rockefeller Center, which opened the same year the Silver Slipper closed. In the film, John Harkrider's set for "Bojangles" looks like part of the Silver Sandal. It was constructed on a separate stage. RKO credited the whole Silver Sandal to Harkrider rather than spoil the illusion.

112

Above and next page: "Never Gonna Dance."

Harkrider was in Hollywood to design the costumes for Universal's *Show Boat* and came to RKO at Kern's suggestion, as did Georges Metaxa, a Roumanian tenor who had sung Victor Florescu in *The Cat and the Fiddle* on the stage. Metaxa was the kind of bad actor who can have one incalculably great moment. The pompous continental bandleader ("Where Ricardo Romero goes, the others come") was it.

Helen Broderick (1890-1959) was the mother of Broderick Crawford and a *diseuse* of reknown on Broadway (Cole Porter wrote "The Tale of an Oyster" for her). She twice played Nurse to Fred and Ginger's Romeo and Juliet, and so well that few people remember her, or her permanent expression of exasperated tolerance, in anything else. In *Swing Time,* she takes them to an inn called the New Amsterdam, after the theater in which she and Astaire had played *The Band Wagon* for 260 performances.

Pandro Berman had decided that George Stevens and Mark Sandrich would take turns directing Astaire-Rogers films. Stevens had much the same RKO background as Sandrich, having made shorts for Lou Brock and a few Wheeler-Woolsey features. He came from a family of actors—his father, Landers Stevens, plays Betty Furness' father in *Swing Time* —and his direction of Katharine Hepburn in *Alice Adams* made it a classic. He could be as slow as Sandrich and somewhat portentous. Toward the close of "Never Gonna Dance" he attempts a daring crane shot but then cuts to a stationary angle at the top of the stairs. It may have been one of the few Astaire-Rogers dances that couldn't be filmed entirely in one continuous shot, for its climax, a spine-chilling series of pirouettes by Rogers, took forty takes to accomplish, and in the middle of shooting Rogers' feet began to bleed.

Shall We Dance

An RKO Radio Picture released May 7, 1937

Producer **Pandro S. Berman** Director **Mark Sandrich** Screenplay **Allan Scott** and **Ernest Pagano** Adaptation **P.J. Wolfson,** based on a story by **Lee Loeb** and **Harold Buchman** Music **George Gershwin** Lyrics **Ira Gershwin** Musical Direction **Nathaniel Shilkret** Ballet Staged by **Hermes Pan** and **Harry Losee** Photography **David Abel** Special Effects **Vernon Walker** Art Director **Van Nest Polglase** Associate Art Director **Carroll Clark** Set Dressing **Darrell Silvera** Miss Rogers' Gowns **Irene** Recording **Hugh McDowell Jr.** Editor **William Hamilton** Running Time 108 minutes

Songs: "Slap That Bass," "Walking the Dog" ("Strictly Instrumental"), "(I've Got) Beginner's Luck," "They All Laughed," "Let's Call the Whole Thing Off," "They Can't Take That Away From Me," "Shall We Dance"

Fred Astaire *Peter P. Peters (Petrov)* **Ginger Rogers** *Linda Keene* **Edward Everett Horton** *Jeffrey Baird* **Eric Blore** *Cecil Flintridge* **Jerome Cowan** *Arthur Miller* **Ketti Gallian** *Denise (Lady Tarrington)* **William Brisbane** *Jim Montgomery* **Frank Moran** *Charlie* **Ann Shoemaker** *Matron* **Harriet Hoctor**

The Film. It would be interesting to know what George Gershwin today would have said of *Shall We Dance*. The songs he composed for it with his brother Ira were not immediate hits, and shortly after the film's release he wrote to a friend in New York: "The picture does not take advantage of the songs as well as it should. They literally throw one or two songs away without any kind of plug. This is mainly due to the structure of the story which does not include any other singers than Fred and Ginger, and the amount of singing one can stand of these two is quite limited." Ira, writing to the same friend, Isaac Goldberg, said, "Maybe it was a mistake to put so many smart songs in one picture." The quotes are from *The Gershwin Years*, by Edward Jablonski and Laurence D. Stewart, and Ira Gershwin today dismisses them. "Looking backward, [mine] seems a rather silly remark. George Gershwin's 'complaint' does not truly reflect our reactions because actually my brother and I were quite happy with *Shall We Dance* and our contributions to it." But there *were* too many smart songs in one picture, "Beginner's Luck" *is* thrown away and "They Can't Take That Away From Me" doesn't get the treatment it deserves.

George Gershwin didn't live long enough to know that many of the songs he wrote for movies in the last years of his life would become standards, and his protest may have stemmed from a momentary rebellion against the difference between writing for the movies and writing for the theater. *Shall We Dance* was the Gershwins' second movie. Their first had been Fox's *Delicious* in 1931; the songs were charming, but none were hits. Movie scores were difficult to write because they had to be short. For their Broadway shows the brothers were used to writing well over a dozen numbers out of which, at their best, they would get perhaps five hits. In the movies they were confined to six or seven numbers, but the movie producers didn't go by the same percentages that Broadway producers did. They wanted all hits. Besides, all the songs had to fit a situation, all had to be tailored to the stars (seldom would subsidiary players get numbers of their own, as often happened in Broadway shows) and, because movies had very limited runs, the score had to produce its hits right

Left: Rogers and Jerome Cowan meet the great Petrov. Above, with Edward Everett Horton: The great Petrov exposed.

away and help promote the picture. Two weeks in a large city was big business; to be "held over" a third week was exceptional. Perhaps this is why, when George Gershwin fell ill, a lot of people thought he was having a nervous breakdown.

The songs in *Shall We Dance* are very good Astaire-type songs. They work nicely in the film, but they aren't planted there as firmly as the songs in *Top Hat* or *Swing Time*—they don't well up out of a dramatic situation, and it's sometimes hard to remember which ones are from this score and which are from *A Damsel in Distress*. The name Gershwin in 1936—the year the brothers were signed by RKO—glowed with prestige; a special aura of "class" surrounded the composer of opera and symphonic works. There's something standoffish about the film; it has an air of silver-dish service that's a little ridiculous. Lift the right cover and you get an honest Fred-and-Ginger number; lift the wrong one and you get Edward Everett Horton or Eric Blore in a dead burlesque routine or Harriet Hoctor in one of her gruesome travesties of ballet. Sometimes there isn't anything underneath at all. This isn't the Gershwins' fault, but it was their hard luck to come in on the series after it had reached its peak and was immovably enthroned upon its laurels—to which now were added the Gershwins.

It was also beginning to use the material that was in circulation around it. Some of it had ceased to circulate, like the junk given to Horton and Blore.

(Was it to make up for his being cut out of *Swing Time* that Blore's scenes were padded so?) The presence of these two immensely likable actors is a link to the series' past, but their material makes it a weak one, like the opulent sets that looked so right in *Top Hat* but looked airless and decadent by 1937. The luxury liner (more luxurious than absolutely necessary), the shipboard kennels and the seasickness jokes are lifted from *Anything Goes,* the Crosby film of 1936. And was it complacency or perversity that ruled out a romantic duet for the stars and put a bad ballet in its place? Yet there's a good side to *Shall We Dance* and, strangely enough, it is in its plot.

Ballet was in the air. It had come to Broadway via Balanchine's choreography in *On Your Toes,* and to Hollywood via Nijinska's in Warner's *A Midsummer Night's Dream* and de Mille's in MGM's *Romeo and Juliet.* The plot of *Shall We Dance* cast Astaire as an American ballet star who dances under a Russian name and who falls in love with Astaire-style dancing and with a Ginger Rogers-style dancer. It projected the dualism of Gershwin's own career (that is, it might have if it hadn't been weakened by casting in the ballet department), and it gave Astaire a motif for his dances. It also contained some imaginative devices that were quite as good as anything in *Swing Time*—better, because they were visual: the flip book of pictures that dissolves into Rogers dancing and the lifesize wax model of Rogers that creates an unearthly effect in one or two scenes. These elements—the ballet vs. musical comedy theme and the real vs. false Ginger theme—are merely stated in the course of the plot; they aren't dramatized and they don't even become themes until the big production number at the end of the film makes them more riotously exciting than we can believe possible. It's as if we'd been walking over a minefield we didn't know was there. But then, isn't that what the plot of a musical should be?

The Numbers. "Beginner's Luck." About one minute of dancing by Astaire, hat and stick in hand, to a phonograph record that repeats itself, and why not? The phonograph is from *The Gay Divorcee* and the dance is a "teaser," just like the one at the start of that film.

"Slap That Bass." More mechanical gadgets for Astaire to play with, in a chromium-plated ship's engine room where the hands and the machinery together make up a perfect rhythm section. Hermes Pan says that Astaire got the idea from a cement mixer on the lot. It may also have been suggested by the machine shop in *Modern Times.* (Chaplin also roller-skated in that film,

as do Astaire and Rogers in "Let's Call the Whole Thing Off." But weren't some of Chaplin's dance steps from *Top Hat*?) Wherever it came from, it's *echt* Astaire and everyone remembers it. But notice how long he stays away from it, how he first uses everything in the situation to feed his invention: tasty bits of jive for the black engineers who are watching are set against caricatured ballet *port de bras*, an arabesque hastily dropped—references to his role in the film as Petrov, reluctant star of the ballet. Only when he's squeezed out the last drop does he proceed to the dance with the machines. (The song is first sung by an unbilled black singer— Mantan Moreland.)

"Walking the Dog." Gershwin wrote a tune and the stars parade up and down with dogs on leashes. This is more teaser and it runs on as if it were a number. It's even reprised as if it were a number, and somewhere there seems to be a highly pleased little voice saying, "See, it's Gershwin and see, they're *not dancing!*" The end of it is Astaire singing "Beginner's Luck," only that, and fadeout. Are they never gonna dance?

"They All Laughed." After she sings it, Rogers allows Astaire to trap her on the dance floor at a rooftop restaurant. He swoops importantly around her in *grands ronds de jambe* and other nonsense. She counters with a burst of tap. He imitates this haltingly, then snaps to. The orchestra begins a vamp and they sail away. The number has everything—games, jokes, hard tap, cool tap, a lovely series of ballet finger turns, and two white pianos to jump onto. Look while you can, because it's the only classic Astaire-Rogers duet in the film.

"Let's Call the Whole Thing Off," the novelty number, takes place in a Central Park rotunda. The set recalls the bandstand in "Isn't This a Lovely Day?" and the "argument" with which the dance begins (she says eether, he says eyether) recalls the tap duologue in "I'll Be Hard to Handle." Here, sitting side by side in their tweeds and wearing roller skates, they clack out their disagreement, haughtily spinning the wheels in the air for emphasis, and the moment when they rise together and strike out across the court is completely unexpected, a musical inspiration typical of Astaire. Another choreographer might have set the moment to the first long move in the music, the "But oh!—" that begins the release. Astaire puts it much earlier, on the last note of the refrain the first time around—literally an "off" moment in the music. We get another marvelous lift from the same effect at the start of the dance to "Let Yourself Go" in *Follow the Fleet*, when he and Rogers sidle onto the dance floor, not to the refrain but to the release, when the band is playing

"Let yourself go—relax and let yourself go."

They tap on those skates, they stagger on those skates, they pump around faster and faster, they go off in "fly" and hit the turf. *Shall We Dance* could have used another dance duet, but this will do very well.

"They Can't Take That Away From Me," one of Gershwin's most beautiful ballads, is most feelingly sung by Fred to Ginger on the ferry from New Jersey, where they have just gone to be married (so that they can be divorced). And then, in the next number, the film makes a catastrophic error: it brings on Harriet Hoctor to dance the reprise with Astaire.

"Shall We Dance" is the theme song of the show staged by Petrov in a merger of Broadway and ballet. He decides that, if he can't dance with Linda Keene, he'll dance with images of her. In the finale Astaire is surrounded by a chorus of girls, each of whom holds a Ginger Rogers mask up to her face. Rogers steps into the lineup and reveals herself for a second. Now Astaire has a Vision Scene, seeking her among the girls. To the racing music of "Shall We Dance" he unmasks them, one after another: wrong, wrong, right, wr—. . . . If this were a romantic ballet, he would have gone on hunting forever, but the music races on in a new key, the lights come up bright, and, after a bit of dancing (a very little bit), the movie ends with "Ho, ho, ho, who's got the last laugh now?"

The working title for this number was "Wake Up and Dance." (Until late in production the film was known, horribly, as *Stepping Toes*.) Gershwin wrote "Shall We Dance" last, along with the ballet music that precedes it, and the number was the last part of the film to be shot. Sandrich tried to get Massine to choreograph the ballet sequence and settled for Harry Losee, whose last assignment had been Sonja Henie's routines in *Thin Ice*. The movie really does wake up and dance: the Ginger chorus wakes it from a nightmare. It's supposed to represent the "Broadway" half of the merger, but it contains more of the fantasy and emotion of ballet than the "ballet," in which turned-in toe dancers rumble around in clumps. The *pas de deux* is set to "They Can't Take That Away From Me." Not even in his satin *premier danseur* tunic can Astaire be taken for a ballet dancer, but Miss Hoctor can be taken for nothing human. She was a contortionist whose specialty, a horseshoe backbend on point, was already well known to movie audiences. (In this position she would kick herself in the head.) Rogers parodies her in some molten backbends of her own that are both amusing and beautiful to see, but by 1937 this kind of primitive,

pseudoaesthetic show dancing was going out of fashion. The very next year, a classical ballet company was brought to the screen when *The Goldwyn Follies* presented Balanchine's American Ballet with Vera Zorina. A pity it couldn't have been Zorina instead of Hoctor in "They Can't Take That Away From Me" and Zorina instead of Ketti Gallian playing the ballerina in the plot (it's really the same character). To say the very least of what that might have led to, the absence of an Astaire-Rogers dance to the ballad would not have struck such a sour note and the ballet would have been interesting in several ways at once. It might even have been interesting enough to stand as Gershwin's one attempt at ballet—he died before he could compose the ballet in *The Goldwyn Follies*. The trouble with *Shall We Dance* was not, as he said, that it didn't have enough singers, but that it didn't have enough dancers.

Production. *Shall We Dance* was a reunion of the Gershwins with Astaire, who had starred in two of their shows on Broadway, and with Rogers, whose last show had been *Girl Crazy*. The Gershwins set to work on a long opening number for Astaire after he tells Horton that he's seen a picture of a marvelous girl and must meet her right away. This they called "Hi-Ho," and Ira's lyric began "Hi-ho! Hi-ho! At last it seems I've found her—Now I won't be happy till my arms are around her." The camera was to follow Astaire as he danced down the street, pausing before posters of Ginger and singing about her to passersby. He winds up at a theater ticket office, and as the shooting script directed, "in the doorway is a portable movie screen upon which is projected Linda doing a whirlwind dance." This image then dissolved into the actual dance of Ginger with her partner. At the last minute the studio decided that the number was too costly to film, so the idea was miniaturized in the form of a flip book that Astaire shows Horton. "Hi-Ho" remained unknown until it was published in 1967.

Another old friend of the Gershwins was Nathaniel Shilkret, music director of RKO. Shilkret had conducted the radio première of "An American in Paris" and had recorded it for RCA Victor. Like Max Steiner before and Victor Baravalle after him, Shilkret conducted but did not himself compose or orchestrate the music heard in the Astaire–Rogers films. The music director delegated these assignments to groups of arrangers, sometimes sketching out themes that he wanted developed in the main titles and underscoring. For the musical numbers, Hal Borne's piano arrangements were the basis of the orchestrations. The dances

"They All Laughed."

were usually filmed to piano tracks recorded by Borne or, if there was time to pre-score and pre-record, orchestral playbacks were used. Astaire always had a number of suggestions to make to the orchestrators, the conductor, the music cutter and the sound men. He would ask for specific orchestral effects under the dancing. Drums were never loud enough for him in a jazz number, and he liked sudden alternations of *pp* and *ff.* One of the men who did a great deal of orchestrating in Astaire-Rogers films was Robert Russell Bennett. Another writer had orchestrated the ballet in *Shall We Dance,* for which Gershwin composed the themes, but after it was recorded and the sequence filmed, Sandrich asked Bennett for a reorchestration. "I had to practically memorize the film," Bennett recalls, "and then I sat down with gallons of coffee and a shot list and worked all night with relays of copyists."

The taps in the dance numbers were recorded on the set during filming, although it was often necessary to re-record them later, for clarity. In the early days when the music was live, there was no way to balance the sound of the music and the taps—they were on the same track. Later there was a tap track apart from the music track, and this could be re-recorded and mixed with sound and music. Astaire would laboriously dub his own taps; Pan would usually dub Rogers'. The dance floors of the films were wood overlaid on the dressier sets with bakelite, which scarred easily. Since shiny floors were part of the décor, the bakelite was kept covered with cardboard during camera rehearsals. Then there would be long waits between takes while the scars were removed with Energine. Oil would have been quicker, but an oiled surface would have been impossible to dance on.

In "Let's Call the Whole Thing Off," Astaire and Rogers skate into medium closeup, then resume the dance in long shot. It's the only such cut I can recall in their numbers (in "Never Gonna Dance," it's a cut on movement). Usually each take would consist of the dance from start to finish, just as it would be done for a live audience. The straight-through take imposed a standard of precision upon performance that was, in Hermes Pan's word, murderous, but it built up a dramatic pressure that was lost later on when choreographers began planning their dances in segments. In the RKO days, the ideal was perfection within a single shot, and to reach it Astaire would shoot all day and often into the night.

The choreography was frontally planned, with full head-to-foot framing—no closeups, no overhead shots. One has the impression of watching every moment

"Let's Call the Whole Thing Off."

from an ideally placed seat in a theater. After "Night and Day," in which Sandrich's camera shot through window blinds and from under tables, the camera angles were reduced to three at most—central field, medium right angle, medium left angle. For most of the RKO series, Astaire set up three cameras to shoot simultaneously; later one camera recorded the whole dance. The dances filmed during 1936-37 suggest that he used both methods. When the camera angle changes, the dance has reached that point in the same or a different take.

For the single-camera method the RKO camera department developed a special vehicle which it called "the Astaire dolly." H.C. Potter, who directed *The Story of Vernon and Irene Castle,* describes it: "It was on tiny wheels with a mount for the camera that put the lens about two feet above the ground. On it rode the camera operator and the assistant who changed the focus and that's all. Fred always wanted to keep the camera in as tight as possible, and they used to shoot with a 40 millimeter lens, which doesn't give you too much leeway. So every time Fred and Ginger moved toward us, the camera had to go back, and every time they moved back, the camera went in. The head grip who was in charge of pushing this thing was a joy to watch. He would maintain a consistent distance, and when they were in the midst of a hectic dance that's quite a stunt."

Astaire suspended his single-shot rule in "Let's Call the Whole Thing Off" because the number was too difficult to film that way. With utmost realism, RKO had poured a concrete floor and there were numerous unscheduled falls. When it was all over and the shooting of the film was nearing its close, Ginger Rogers and Alfred Gwynne Vanderbilt Jr. threw a mammoth roller-skating party at a local rink. *Le tout* Hollywood came in its old clothes, and *Life* approvingly informed its readers: "Extraordinary among Hollywood parties, this one was so much fun that few guests got drunk."

Next page: The Ginger chorus in "Shall We Dance."

Change Partners

For the first time in three years there was no Astaire–Rogers fall release. Instead there was *Stage Door* with Ginger Rogers and Katharine Hepburn (released October 8, 1937) and *A Damsel in Distress* with Fred Astaire and Joan Fontaine (released November 19, 1937). The long-expected break had come at last; it would be a full fifteen months before Astaire and Rogers appeared together again on the screen.

Astaire's preparations for a musical were voluminous. Going at top speed he could not produce more than two a year, and Rogers was prevented by the long and wearying rehearsal periods from competing for roles with actresses who were not making musicals. In 1936 Carole Lombard had three films in release; Jean Arthur, five; Myrna Loy, six. In 1935, the first year of the series, Rogers' role in it was not so large, and she broke away for two films without Astaire. She had no inordinate dramatic ambitions at this time and often spoke of one of these films, *Star of Midnight*, as an example of the kind of thing she liked to do. It was a comedy-thriller with William Powell as a suave detective, much like his films with Loy. Rogers made it right after *Roberta* and it was a big success, but neither it nor *In Person*, which she did after *Top Hat*, erased the public's impression of her as Fred Astaire's girl. In some ways *In Person* enhanced it.

It was a very minor musical with songs by Oscar Levant and Dorothy Fields, and it was built entirely around Rogers. The point of it was to lift her out of the co-star category, but it was too slight to do more than suggest the bigger things she would go on to in the next two Astaire films. She played a movie star who puts on disguises (black wig, buck teeth) to run away from crowds. Escaping sordid fame in a simple mountain retreat, she's crushed when a simple mountaineer (George Brent) doesn't seem to recognize her. William Seiter directed in a casual sunny style and Hermes Pan furnished the choreography. Rogers' charm was irresistible, her skill variable. In one number, wearing a pinafore and whipping up something in the kitchen, she hears her own voice singing "Got a New Lease on Life" over the radio. "That's *me!*" she cries, and in a rapture of self-intoxication dances around the house. Then she goes ersatz in "Out of Sight, Out of Mind," slinking with a studiously lighted cigarette among men in dinner jackets, looking like a junior miss caught out in Ladies' Evening Wear. Yet only a year later she was the cream of sophistication in "Let's Face the Music and Dance." The difference: Astaire.

After filming one of the dances in *Follow the Fleet*, Rogers told a reporter

that she wanted to take a vacation "digging mines." Astaire was notably grouchy on the subject of his partnership with Rogers, and Pandro Berman has said that he had repeatedly to force the two of them together. Personal enmity was not the reason, professional pride was. The same pride that kept them locked together in a cycle of hits, their teamwork getting better and better, made each of them ever more eager to succeed without the other. There was something comic in their predicament: Astaire had forged for himself a new romantic style in the movies, a style that had made people forget he was Adele's brother, and in the forging of it had created a new menace to his own survival. Would they ever forget he was Ginger Rogers' partner? Here was Ginger, who had made Astaire's transition possible, not really a developed dancer and an only modest singer who had turned from brass to gold under his touch; here was Ginger, still uncertain whether she was a star or not, seeing her career rushing to an end—"all washed up at thirty"—with a smile and a song. The comedy of this was unperceived by the public at large; eighty million people a week saw only success. Like Hilaire Belloc's barbarians, they watched from beyond, and on their faces there was no smile. In later years Astaire and Rogers issued dozens of warm and gracious statements about one another, statements that probably are accurate reflections of their tenderest feelings at the time of the partnership, but none of these has quite offset the public's belief, formed at the time, that their success was an ordeal of the bitch-goddess kind. There is something in mass adulation that wants the comfort of a moral to the success story. Success is easier for the unsuccessful when it has a core of unhappiness and bitter sacrifice and harsh bad feelings. The stories about the hard work that Fred and Ginger put into their dancing weren't enough. Fred and Ginger had also to hate each other. We turn to the fan magazines, to the back pages of the program, looking to have exposed what we've just seen in the spotlight—we want it to be not just an illusion but a lie. And there's an element of titillation, too, in the suggestion that a glorious romantic duet can be performed with curses snarled through clenched teeth.

Rumors of a breakup raged anew in 1936, when the studio renegotiated its contracts with Astaire and Rogers. To put pressure on Rogers the studio let out stories that she would be replaced (its most egregious candidate was Carole Lombard, at a figure topping her Paramount salary; others were Margo, Ruby Keeler and Jessie Matthews), but no one seems to have believed them. She did get one of the things she wanted most—more pictures away from

Astaire. In the period between *Shall We Dance* and *Carefree* she turned out three movies to his one, and her career soared. She became, with Hepburn, Lombard, Arthur, Loy, Colbert and Dunne, one of the screen's top comediennes.

For both Rogers and Hepburn, it was *Stage Door* that did it. Hepburn had had a string of flops after *Alice Adams,* and Berman conceived the idea of teaming her with RKO's other queen, Rogers, in a light modern comedy about struggling actresses in New York. The script, from a bad Ferber-Kaufman play, was remade from the ground up and shot pretty much off the cuff. Adolphe Menjou played a producer with a fully tenanted casting couch, and the supporting cast included Lucille Ball, Eve Arden, Gail Patrick, Ann Miller, Jack Carson, Franklin Pangborn and Grady Sutton. There were a number of not too recondite in-jokes: Constance Collier as an elder gorgon of the stage equally available for coaching or comebacks; the line "the calla lilies are in bloom again," taken from *The Lake,* a play in which Hepburn had bombed in New York two seasons before, and used as part of the play-within-the-movie, "Enchanted April," which got its name from an RKO disaster of 1935 with Ann Harding. The reputed feud between Rogers and Hepburn was exploited with great good humor. They play roommates,

In Person: *"Out of Sight, Out of Mind."*

With Katharine Hepburn in Stage Door.

and when rich-girl Hepburn moves in with her pyramid of luggage, Rogers says, "Why don't we just sleep in the hall? No sense crowding the trunks." Rogers was pseudotough, scared, a fighter and a loser. Hepburn was a starry-eyed rebel, indomitably in love with the thea-tah. When the two of them clashed, it was with an underlying respect, and it was always Rogers who attacked, Hepburn who parried. (In Hepburn's later screen relationship with Tracy, it was much the same, with Hepburn taking the offensive.)

Rogers' role as Jean Maitland was next to nonexistent in the original. The director, Gregory La Cava, and the writers, Morrie Ryskind and Anthony Veiller, created the character for her. They kept the better half of the Terry Randall role for Hepburn and pushed the smarmier traits onto Andrea Leeds, who played the suicide. The death of Leeds is as melodramatic a set piece as any young boarding-house ham could wish for; at times the film sees life and the theater through the eyes of the girls, and it gets pretty blubbery toward the end. But most of the lines are still as hard and funny, the manic-depressive dormitory atmosphere as true, the feminine microcosm as appealing, as they undoubtedly seemed in 1937, when La Cava won a New York Film Critics

Circle prize for direction. He made two more films with Rogers, *Fifth Avenue Girl* (1939) and *The Primrose Path* (1940).

In a much-quoted, typical-Thirties aphorism, Katharine Hepburn had said of Rogers and Astaire, "He gives her class and she gives him sex." *A Damsel in Distress* was as sexless as a sewing basket, but it went double on class: a Wodehouse book (the real thing this time, not a derivation like *The Gay Divorcee*), a hypersophisticated Gershwin score, a gracious English manor setting and the pearliest photography yet seen in a musical. In the cast were George Burns and Gracie Allen, Reginald Gardiner, Ray Noble, Constance Collier and Montagu Love. About all it didn't have was an adequate dance partner for Astaire, and it was his first flop.

English-bred Joan Fontaine played the sequestered Lady Alyce of Totleigh Castle, who dreams of the American who will come to rescue her. Improbable as it may seem, the role was once projected for Ginger Rogers. (It was a period when she was also being announced for things like *Irene* and *Mother Carey's Chickens.*) When the box-office receipts for *Swing Time* showed a slight falling off, RKO agreed to break up the team temporarily and, after a search, is said to have settled on contract player Fontaine because as a nondancer she wouldn't invite comparisons with Rogers. Only twenty years old and still gauche as an actress, she wore a fixed smile of pain through the entire movie. One sees why in her one nondance with Astaire, "Things Are Looking Up," performed as they wander through a park. The director, George Stevens, hurls so many treetrunks between her and the lens that she looks worse than she is, and, as she and Astaire cross a pond, he cuts away from her in midleap, so that she appears to be taking a header into the water.

Astaire is alone for three of the numbers. He sings "A Foggy Day" in that same park, with Joseph August's filtered photography making great hosannas of the rolling banks of fog. To take the place of the big duet at the end of the film he dances and plays a variety of percussion instruments to "Nice Work If You Can Get It." "I Can't Be Bothered Now" is to me the most Astaire-sounding song in the two film scores that the Gershwins wrote for him. Its rendition in the movie is a little disappointing though it is pictorially splendid: Astaire on a London street with traffic rolling by in the background raps out a few choruses, swings his umbrella and, much too soon, catches a bus. (The staging may have been suggested by *Shall We Dance*'s aborted "Hi-Ho.")

The score of *Damsel* is laced with mock-English whimsey that occasionally

becomes as twee as the plot. "The Jolly Tar and the Milkmaid," sung by Astaire and two lady madrigalists at Totleigh Castle, and "Sing of Spring," played but not performed, are in this vein. The best of the "English" numbers is "Stiff Upper Lip," sung by Gracie Allen at the entrance to a fun house. Burns and Allen are like ministering angels in this film; they're so needed and they're so good. Both danced well, and Gracie could even dance in character. Like Ginger Rogers she tap-danced without losing her femininity. The fun house sequence, for which Hermes Pan won an Oscar, is elaborate and inventive, with much use of distorting mirrors, treadmills, revolving drums and staircases that turn into chutes. Its high point is Gracie Allen endlessly jogging in circles on a turning disc. This was based on the "Oompah Trot" that Fred and Adele Astaire had used as a trademark exit in five of their shows. It consisted of a steady trot shoulder-to-shoulder around and around the stage, with the band playing oompahs until the Astaires trotted off, invariably to return for an encore.

Burns and Allen dance with Astaire in one other number for which there is no vocal. The music might be the "Put Me to the Test" written by Gershwin for this film. The lyric wasn't used until Gene Kelly sang it in *Cover Girl* to an entirely new musical setting by Jerome Kern.

Astaire's big solo is certainly the dance highlight of the film, as it would be of almost any film. He dances it entirely in a small triangular space surrounded by drums of every description. It was the ultimate expression of the one-man revolution that he had started in "A Needle in a Haystack." In the Forties when his career was in one of its infrequent lulls, he was unfavorably compared to Gene Kelly for not getting the most out of the film medium. The critics missed the point. Astaire could always give more to the film medium than he could get out of it. When he experimented with the capacities of film it was usually in order to give more of himself—shadows of Astaire, mirror reflections of Astaire. In "Nice Work If You Can Get It," he gives himself and his virtuosity as the irreducible elements of spectacle. He neither moves out nor moves the camera, and the number is a vest-pocket hurricane.

Astaire's means and his style were not available to imitators, but he was technically the greatest revolutionary in the history of the movie musical. He forced camerawork, cutting, synchronization and scoring to ever higher standards of sensitivity and precision. He fought on every front, and in the cutting room he was a terror. When Astaire arrived in Hollywood, almost the first thing he did was dispense with the reaction shots that would be cut into a

A Damsel in Distress. *Below: With Joan Fontaine. Right: "The Jolly Tar and the Milkmaid." The lady on Astaire's right is the great Jan Duggan of W.C. Fields films.*

dance (he allowed one in "The Carioca"). And no one until that time had insisted on so exact a synchronization of picture and sound. Astaire could detect disparities where everyone else saw wholeness and perfection. He would say to the editor, "Move the film two sprocket holes ahead." (Film moves at the speed of 24 frames a second and there are perhaps four sprocket holes per frame.) Then he would look at the result as it flashed through the Moviola and say, "No, maybe one."

Although Ginger Rogers had, in the course of the Astaire series, acquired all the polish she would ever need as a star, the studio now cast her in a series of social-underdog parts that *characterized* her as a star. In *Vivacious Lady*, directed by George Stevens and released in the spring of 1938, she played a nightclub singer whom James Stewart smuggles home to his formidably conventional upper-class parents. A few months later, in *Having Wonderful Time*, she was a secretary who meets Douglas Fairbanks Jr. on a vacation. *Vivacious Lady* had undertones of a slapstick *Alice Adams*, but the class conflict was buried beneath layers of intricately webbed will-they-won't-they-get-to-bed sex farce. In *Having Wonderful Time*, directed by Alfred Santell from Arthur Kober's stories of Jewish resort life in the Catskills, Fairbanks was the poor boy working his way through college who laughs at Rogers' dreams of marrying a rich man. Then, in the next film with Astaire, a new element was added to the Ginger Rogers character that had nothing to do with social status but that mysteriously completed it and made it a part of the mythology of an era.

137

Carefree

An RKO Radio Picture released September 2, 1938

Producer **Pandro S. Berman** Director **Mark Sandrich** Screenplay **Allan Scott** and **Ernest Pagano** Story and Adaptation **Dudley Nichols** and **Hagar Wilde** Music and Lyrics **Irving Berlin** Musical Direction **Victor Baravalle** Ensembles Staged by **Hermes Pan** Photography **Robert de Grasse** Special Effects **Vernon L. Walker** Art Director **Van Nest Polglase** Associate Art Director **Carroll Clark** Set Dressing **Darrell Silvera** Miss Rogers' Gowns **Howard Greer** Wardrobe **Edward Stevenson** Assistant Director **Argyle Nelson** Editor **William Hamilton** Recording **Hugh McDowell Jr.** Running Time 83 minutes

Songs: "Since They Turned 'Loch Lomond' into Swing," "I Used to Be Color-Blind," "The Yam," "Change Partners," "The Night Is Filled with Music" (instrumental background)

Fred Astaire *Dr. Tony Flagg* **Ginger Rogers** *Amanda Cooper* **Ralph Bellamy** *Stephen Arden* **Luella Gear** *Aunt Cora* **Jack Carson** *Connors* **Clarence Kolb** *Judge Joe Travers* **Franklin Pangborn** *Roland Hunter* **Walter Kingsford** *Dr. Powers* **Kay Sutton** *Miss Adams* **Tom Tully** *Policeman* **Hattie McDaniel** *Maid* **Robert B. Mitchell and the St. Brendan's Boys Choir**

"I Used to Be Color-Blind."

Treating "complex maladjustment" with Walter Kingsford.

The Film. *Carefree* is more screwball comedy than musical, and it is more Ginger Rogers' film than Fred Astaire's. It's also the shortest of the Astaire-Rogers films, with only four numbers, and an obstacle course of a plot that clearly was never intended to support a musical. However, the script was worked around somehow, and here, as straight as I can tell it, is the story:

Humorless young attorney Ralph Bellamy is desperate because Rogers, a singing star of radio, can't make up her mind to marry him, so he has her analyzed by his good friend Astaire, a psychiatrist who practices with a white-coated anesthetist (Jack Carson) and a lab full of optical instruments. In his office, she overhears a diagnosis (uncomplimentary) of his last patient, thinks he's talking about her and resists treatment. Bellamy gets them both out to his country club where, after doing a dance on the golf links, the doctor orders up a large meal of bizarre dishes that will induce his patient to dream. She dreams a slow-motion duet with the doctor ("I Used to Be Color Blind") and wakes up in love with him. The next morning he tells her that there's nothing really the matter with her, so to hold his interest she makes up a dream that causes him to pronounce her "the most beautiful case of complex maladjustment." To free her of any lingering inhibitions he gives her an anesthetic, and, in an unguarded moment, she walks out of the building and runs amok, kicking policemen, throwing a nightstick through a sheet of plate glass and savaging her sponsor's product on the air. That night at the country club dance, she threatens to hurl more objects unless he dances with her. They do "The Yam."

There follows a scene, possibly the most touching one ever played by Astaire and Rogers, in which she weeps quietly while he tells her that all patients fall in love with their analysts. He now hypnotizes her, planting the idea that she loves the stuffy lawyer, that she doesn't love the dancing doctor and that all men like himself should be shot. (The script's peculiarly nasty phrase is "shot down like dogs.") Again she runs amok, driving wildly through the streets to Bellamy's side at the country club, where a skeet shoot is in progress, and

when Dr. Flagg arrives, she grabs a gun and shoots up the place. Meanwhile, Flagg consults his own unconscious (a two-way conversation in a mirror), finds that he's really in love with the girl and attempts to get through to her on the dance floor that night. This is "Change Partners": "Must you dance/Ev'ry dance/With the same/Fortunate man?" Rogers is dancing with Bellamy, Astaire with Luella Gear, who plays Rogers' maiden aunt. Astaire sings over his shoulder: "Ask him to sit this one out and while you're alone/I'll tell the waiter to tell him he's wanted on/The telephone. . . ." And he asks Jack Carson to phone Bellamy from a booth in the lobby, which Carson does in a falsetto squawk as "Miss Setsumi Naguchi, editor of a woman's column for the Honolulu *Daily Bugle.*" Alone on the patio, Rogers is lured instantly into a trance by Astaire, but before he can speak, Bellamy rushes in and snatches her away. The two men are now enemies, and the doctor is barred from the country club. Carson, dispatched with some knock-out drops, gets the wrong Miss Cooper—Luella Gear (she invites him in when he says, "I'm going to give you something that'll make you feel real nice")—and the wedding goes on

Standard movie satire of the Thirties and Forties: commercial radio show wrecked by its star.

as scheduled, with Rogers' unconscious mind still telling her she hates Astaire. However, there's a last-minute scramble: Astaire breaks in, Bellamy swings at him and knocks out the bride. The wedding comes off with Astaire in Bellamy's place and Rogers with one black eye.

With nearly everyone in Hollywood under analysis in 1938, you'd think *Carefree* would have hit its target at least some of the time, just as you'd expect *Shall We Dance*, a musical about professional theatrical dancing, to have shown a less crippling naiveté about ballet. It's Ginger Rogers who carries most of the "spoof" material, and though she doesn't, in her scenes of mayhem, bring it to much more than a calculated cuteness (how mechanical, after all, was that late-Thirties tradition of lady stars kicking up their heels), she's oddly compelling in that double way of hers; she's like a clever puppy who knows it's being watched. Her dancing often had the same fascination on a higher—the highest—plane. She loved to act and she loved to play-act, to sustain both a character and that character's ego-centered fantasy life. Her best acting was a form of double imposture, masquerade on top of performance, and her best characters were women whose lives were an act: the softies who put up a tough front, the secretaries and salesgirls who saw themselves as rich and glamorous, who were nobody's fools except their own.

Almost any Ginger Rogers role is successful to the degree that it reflects the dualism in her personality (tough-vulnerable, ingenuous-calculating) or plays on her curious aptitude for mimicry or fantasy or imposture. She needs guises the way other actresses need closeups, and it's revealing that, although she never did play the dual roles she seems to have been cut out for, she was the only movie actress of the sound era who appeared regularly as a child. In 1940 she won an Oscar for *Kitty Foyle*, the soapiest of the working-girl fables, but the classic Ginger Rogers character was formed by a marriage of screwball comedy and fairy tales. She was the sleepwalker in the bridal veil, the working-class princess with the millionaire waiting at the church. She didn't know her own mind, could never choose among her men. In *Tom, Dick and Harry*, bells rang in her head to tell her which of her three suitors (Burgess Meredith, George Murphy and Alan Marshall) was Mr. Right. The tumbled state of her psyche is the most real thing in *Carefree*; and when she goes into one of her trances, it's like seeing a rehearsal for the classic roles that were to come: the brilliant flight of *Tom, Dick and Harry*, the terrible crash of *Lady in the Dark*.

"The Yam." Following page: The Yam Lift. The table against which Astaire braces his foot is missing from this still.

"Ginger Rogers Dreaming" might be the title
of some essay on the iconography of the Forties,
and with more spark and less fluff *Tom, Dick
and Harry* might have been the definitive portrait
of a certain kind of innocent all-American bitch.
It's halfway to being that already, and Liza Elliott
in *Lady in the Dark* is halfway to being that same
character ten years later (after the quick divorce
from Burgess Meredith). Liza can't make up her
mind either—she even sings a song about it, "The
Saga of Jenny"—and, of course, she's in analysis.
Rogers got bad notices for presuming to take on
a role that Gertrude Lawrence had done on the
stage, but there's very little of Gertrude Lawrence
in the movie version. Instead there's a tense and
troubled Rogers (a *tense* Rogers is a contradic-
tion in terms) struggling hopelessly with the most
lugubrious conception of her character to date.
All the elements were there—the wedding, the
dream sequences, the kid act, even the three
suitors were there—and most of them had been
in the show. The movie didn't "distort" Moss
Hart's book. But it did distort the Ginger character: the brash sexual egotism that made the heroine of *Tom, Dick and Harry* so awesome and so
funny—you felt that no man could possibly love
her more than she loved herself—became a kind
of chilly narcissism, the screwball became a walking identity crisis in tight hairdos and dun-colored
suits, and instead of being alluring and potent in
her dreams she was garish and monstrous. Ginger
Rogers *was* the Lady in the Dark, but by the time
the character came back to her as Liza Elliott in
1944, the dopey spoof-psychiatry of *Carefree* had
been replaced by the pretentious, solicitous, load-
ed symbolism of popularized Freud. This was
the "sophisticated" version of Ginger Rogers

and a mess of a movie. Though a commercial success, it was a disaster in Rogers' career equivalent to that of *Yolanda and the Thief* in Astaire's. *Yolanda*, released the following year, has at least a rococo charm, and Astaire survived it. But after *Lady in the Dark* there was nothing left of the Rogers character. She died on the analyst's couch.

Although *Carefree* contains more than its share of novelties, it is very much the twilight movie of the Astaire-Rogers series. The wheel of the Thirties had turned and the Forties are already here, in the clothes that Rogers wears—the splashy appliqués, the witch hats, the snoods—and in the muted luxury of the settings: white wood and fieldstone for the country club and its grounds, with only now and then a satin chair or fluted drape echoing the "streamlined" urban glitter of the earlier films. The lighting is lower-key and the photography is softer (the cameraman was now Robert de Grasse, Rogers' favorite). Much of the film is shot out of doors; it breathes of freshly turned earth. But there was no new planting. This really was the end.

The Numbers. "Since They Turned 'Loch Lomond' into Swing" is one of Astaire's merriest as well as one of his most fiendishly versatile solos. He dances Scottish fashion over two golf clubs crossed on the ground, then tees off some half-dozen balls in rhythm, pausing only for a fast shuffle between strokes. Each ball is straight as a shot. Anything else? He plays the harmonica while dancing. This number is among Astaire's own favorites. There is no vocal.

"I Used to Be Color-Blind" is a short floating duet in a mock pastoral setting and a total surprise—not just because it's in slow motion but because so much of it takes place in the air. There are supported jumps for Rogers, a lift from which she's lowered in a spiral and a long tandem leap across a brook. Astaire customarily avoided lifts. *Carefree* is full of them. Normally he partnered Rogers with one arm like steel around her waist, but in this film she hovers at his fingertips or is whirled about him in space. She takes the exposure marvelously, a point lavishly emphasized by the slow motion in "Color-Blind."

Much was made of the long kiss that ends this sequence because kisses were not in the Astaire-Rogers tradition (any more than lifts were). Astaire in his flying tails, the pliant Rogers in one of her less-is-more gowns, were an erotic vision that audiences beheld in the electric silence of the dance. Everyone knew what was happening in these dances, yet everyone enjoyed being teased about it, too. The films usually contained some business about a kiss that doesn't

come off or that we don't see, but there was a significant moment of "afterglow," following the big dance, that we did see. *Carefree,* the together-again film after the fifteen-month separation, broke several traditions at once. The stars went on kissing, and lifting, in *The Castles.*

"The Yam." People were doing the Big Apple and the Lambeth Walk, and they probably did the Yam Strut up the aisles and out of the movie theaters, but the rest of the dance is superhuman. The staging is also something special. "The Yam" starts on the country club dance floor and, as the camera pulls back and crowds of guests follow along, it moves down the room and out of the building onto a brick path, turns a corner and comes back inside, gathers momentum as it crosses a lounge full of stuffed chairs into which Fred bounces Ginger, and winds up back on the dance floor, where it climaxes in a splendid series of flying lifts around the room. At the same time that Astaire's solos became more ingenious in their use of confined space, his duets began to eat up the landscape. "The Yam" is an extension of "I Used to Be Color-Blind" and the sadly botched "Things Are Looking Up" of *A Damsel in Distress* — expansive, traveling dances in which "the world's our ballroom" is more than just a sentiment. And the sensational Yam Lift has a touch of the famous tabletop dance at the end of *The Gay Divorcee*: Astaire props his foot up on the ringside tables and swings Rogers over his leg. (Hermes Pan, whose idea this was, used it again with Betty Grable in *Sweet Rosie O'Grady.* And Irving Berlin took the melodic phrase "Any Yam today?" and used it in "Any Bonds Today?", a song written in 1941 for the U.S. Treasury Department.)

"Change Partners." Astaire for the first time doesn't play the part of a dancer. He's strangely convincing as a psychoanalyst in the same way that Danny Kaye used to be convincing as a hypochondriac. As a hypnotist Astaire is quick and delicate with intelligent hands; the whole improbable idea becomes lyrical. Rogers is his ideal subject. When she cries in the plot of the movie, she's affecting because it's unusual for her defenses to be so far relaxed. And when Astaire rules her movements in the trance dance, that little division in her nature interests us all over again, only now it dissolves completely in an unchecked surrender of her will. "Change Partners," like "Let's Face the Music and Dance," is just on the edge of being absurd, and, though it isn't as great a dance number, it may be a greater demonstration of personal force in the projection of a drama—and it hasn't even a show-within-a-show rationale to protect it. "Change Partners" is Fred and Ginger working without a net.

147

Astaire hypnotizes Rogers in "Change Partners."

At the end they do one of their spiralling lifts with Rogers falling far backward in a tranquil arc, her arms wreathed over her head. The way she holds her poses in the air without "posing" is one of the loveliest things about *Carefree*. Her dancing was always strict in that way and it hasn't dated, as Jessie Matthews' and Eleanor Powell's have, because it's so refreshingly laconic. It was dancing at its driest and shapeliest; it had none of the excesses, nothing of the sweet tooth of its period. And though half the time in the slow duets we're contemplating the beauty of her body, we can see that it's also an expressive body—that the back is strong and whiplike as well as beautifully molded, the waist long and sinuous, the hips free, the chest open. Feet and hands are delicious. The famous T-square shoulders are troublesome because they have too much force in turns where her balance was chancey, and because what little tension she showed tended to collect there. What little modishness also. Loosely settled,

as they often are, they're ideal. She can lift her arms high from this broad yoke and create a glorious "portrait" frame for her head. (Another lovely frame: the "brackets," with squared elbows.)

In *Carefree* Rogers' dancing is up to her peak performances in *Follow the Fleet* and *Swing Time*. She had returned glowingly to the series, and the movie features the new independent Rogers in the dances as well as in the plot. And yet the partnership seems more solid than ever. Astaire and Rogers never stopped proving themselves. In this film they even seem to have reached a new understanding of each other, a new intimacy and confidence in their dancing and in their scenes together, as if they were at that stage in a relationship when friends feel they've just begun to get acquainted.

Production.

Sandrich managed, just barely, to squeeze a musical out of the script. The screenplay was based on material by Dudley Nichols and Hagar Wilde, the RKO team that had written one of the year's better screwball comedies, *Bringing Up Baby*, in which Fritz Feld as a twitchy psychiatrist does in about fifteen seconds what *Carefree* fails to do in its eighty-three minutes. Sandrich's writers were now Allan Scott and Ernest Pagano, with Pagano supplying the main jokes and sight gags—e.g. Rogers breaking the plate glass in *Carefree*. One of their opening scenes, a session between Astaire and a giddy patient played by Grace Hayle, was cut out of the film.

There were no substantial cuts made in *Carefree*. "The Night Is Filled with Music," a Berlin song projected for the dream duet, was never filmed. The song is heard as instrumental background, and "I Used to Be Color Blind" was used instead. Berlin's lyric was written for color ("the red in your cheeks, the gold in your hair, the blue in your eyes"), and at one point in the dance the image was supposed to go from black and white into color. When color tests turned out badly, the idea was dropped.

Even if the stars had wanted to continue as a team, RKO no longer had the talent or the means to put original vehicles together. At the end of 1938, after having undergone five years of reorganization, the company was again facing bankruptcy. Its biggest year financially had been 1936, the year that Astaire and Rogers rose highest in the exhibitors' polls. In 1937, with only one release, they dropped to seventh place, and in 1938 they dropped out of the Top Ten. At the same time, contracts were running out. Sandrich had a money fight with the studio, although ostensibly the fight was over a film

called *The Joy of Living* that Pandro Berman wanted him to direct. (It was a Kern semimusical, rather like *Carefree* in style, starring Irene Dunne and Douglas Fairbanks Jr. Tay Garnett eventually directed.) Unlike Berman, Berlin and Astaire, Sandrich had never received a percentage of the profits on his RKO films, and after *Carefree* he left to form his own unit at Paramount. In 1942 he had his biggest hit since Astaire-Rogers days, *Holiday Inn,* with Bing Crosby singing "White Christmas" and Astaire dancing "Say It With Firecrackers." He was preparing *Blue Skies* in 1945 when he suddenly died of a heart attack at the age of forty-four.

All of the Astaire-Rogers films made money; the inclusive figure that was quoted at the end of 1938 was $18 million. Several of the early ones were reissued, and that happened to only a handful of the big hits of the Thirties. *Carefree* and *The Story of Vernon and Irene Castle* made less money than the others. They were a "different" kind of Astaire-Rogers movie, and as an Irving Berlin show *Carefree* was somewhat overshadowed by Fox's *Alexander's Ragtime Band.* It was also more Rogers and Astaire than Astaire and Rogers. At the end of the year RKO considered Rogers its No. 1 star and began laying plans for a straight dramatic career, while Astaire ran out his contract.

Wedding Day. With Jack Carson in his first sizable role, Ralph Bellamy type-cast as the stuffy suitor, and Luella Gear, the original Hortense of Gay Divorce.

The Castles in The Sunshine Girl, *1913. Facing page: The Castle Walk, with Ginger Rogers in an adaptation of Irene Castle's costume, including the famous Dutch cap.*

The Story of Vernon and Irene Castle

An RKO Radio Picture released April 7, 1939

Produced by **George Haight** and **Pandro S. Berman** Director **H.C. Potter** Screenplay by **Richard Sherman, Oscar Hammerstein II** and **Dorothy Yost,** based on *My Husband* and *My Memories* by **Irene Castle** Musical Direction **Victor Baravalle** Ensembles by **Hermes Pan** Photography **Robert de Grasse** Special Effects **Vernon L. Walker** Montage **Douglas Travers** Set Dressing **Darrell Silvera** Art Director **Van Nest Polglase** Associate Art Director **Perry Ferguson** Costumes **Walter Plunkett** and **Edward Stevenson** Miss Rogers' Gowns **Irene Castle** Assistant Director **Argyle Nelson** Editor **William Hamilton** Sound Recording **Richard Van Hessen** Running Time 90 minutes

Songs: "Only When You're in My Arms" by **Con Conrad**, **Bert Kalmar** and **Harry Ruby** plus the following songs performed by Astaire and Rogers: "The Yama Yama Man," "By the Light of the Silvery Moon," "Waiting for the Robert E. Lee," "Too Much Mustard," (Castle Walk), "Rose Room" (Tango), "Little Brown Jug" (Polka), "Dengozo" (Maxixe), "Who's Your Lady Friend?" "Millicent Waltz," "Night of Gladness," "Missouri Waltz"

Fred Astaire *Vernon Castle* **Ginger Rogers** *Irene Castle* **Edna May Oliver** *Maggie Sutton* **Walter Brennan** *Walter Ash* **Lew Fields** *Lew Fields* **Etienne Giradot** *Papa Aubel* **Rolfe Sedan** *Emile Aubel* **Janet Beecher** *Mrs. Foote* **Robert Strange** *Dr. Foote* **Leonid Kinskey** *Artist* **Clarence Derwent** *Papa Louis* **Victor Varconi** *Grand Duke* **Frances Mercer** *Claire Ford* **Donald MacBride** *Hotel Manager* **Douglas Walton** *Student Pilot* **Sonny Lamont** *Charlie the tap dancer*

With Lew Fields.

The Film. When Fred Astaire first scored in the movies, millions of Americans reached into their French vocabularies for the adjectives that seemed to fit him uniquely: debonair, nonchalant, insouciant. The same words had been applied twenty years before to Mr. and Mrs. Vernon Castle. Insouciance, *sans souci* = *Carefree*; in 1914 the Sans Souci was the Castles' supper club in Times Square. They had their success first in Paris, dancing an American importation, the Grizzly Bear or the Texas Tommy, in a French revue of 1912, and repeating it nightly to ovations at the Café de Paris. Paris was in a fever over American ragtime. It was the way the Castles performed the new social dances from America—the Bunny Hug, the Turkey Trot, the One-Step (which they rechristened the Castle Walk)—that made their European reputation. Their style was casual, light, simple, and, best of all, spontaneous. In America they helped sweep away what remained of the systematic, organized European ballroom dances of the nineteenth century (the quadrille, the Lancers, the German—those now oppressive tokens of a now insecure leisure class). They gave the waltzes and polkas and gavottes a new insolence, and they made the rowdy new popular dances respectable, releasing high society from the indignity of slumming and opening a new safety lane to the upwardly mobile sons and daughters of the middle class. For with the dances and dance lessons came codes of etiquette, habits of dress and a whole new standard of chic, informal, improvised, even silly, that could be assimilated by people without money. Wristwatches for men. Jewelry for men. For women *no* jewelry. Bobbed hair, flowing dresses without corsets, lapdogs carried in the street. All of it came stamped with the Castle trademark, along with a host of products—shoes and cigars and toiletries—bearing their name.

Catalysts and popularizers rather than reformers or innovators, the Castles were perhaps the first large expression of modern mass society and its cult

of good taste, its How To lessons, its obsession with The Correct Thing. Old social barriers that had defended "taste" and confined it to the wealthy were crumbling. Now, on all levels of society but the lowest, The Correct Thing was simply what the Castles did, two fine dancers with a sense of the moment and a flair for self-promotion. Their mixture of common sense and frivolity, of youthful exuberance and refinement, were what the early teens of the century demanded. They fused the decorum of the mansion ballroom and the vitality of the streets; they were proper and they were gay. Their reign was short, flourishing in that brief twinkle of the world's eye between the end of the Mauve Decade and the start of the war. Vernon was killed in 1918. But through them masses of Americans discovered their dances and their dance music, their democratic right to elegance and the pursuit of fun.

Nothing is harder to convey than the impact of a change that has been universally accepted. The whole social backdrop is missing from *The Story of Vernon and Irene Castle*. The shift from a stratified to a homogenous "polite" society and the emergence of the genuinely native popular music to which the Castles danced aren't touched upon for the same reason: the novel had become the norm. For more than a generation Americans had danced to the rapidly changing forms of "syncopated" music. It was hard to remember that there had ever been any other kind, and in the Thirties the norm had been recrystallized in the person of Fred Astaire. What most Americans had done for recreation Astaire did with the insuperable dedication of a lifelong professional. His career had been nurtured by the progression of ragtime to jazz to swing (to use the terms applied by successive eras to the same kind of music), and the first major formative situation in which he found himself was the period dominated by the Castles. Astaire was fourteen when, with Adele, he saw them in *The Sunshine Girl* nine times. The Astaires, though well on their way (they'd been on the stage for eight years), were among the innumerable legatees of the Castle style. More than any other entertainer Astaire bears the imprint of those incredibly confident, innocent prewar years. He epitomized the classless "aristocratic" American of the Thirties, and it is with an ever more anguished sense of his increasing isolation that we have clung to him ever since.

For their last film Astaire and Rogers danced without passion and without mystery, as sweethearts or as husband and wife, but not as lovers. They gave up their own dances and did these excellent pastiches or reconstructions, less genteel than the originals, but also less faddish. Irene Castle, who was hired

Left above: The Foote family holds Vernon Castle prisoner for a performance by Irene. Walter Brennan, Janet Beecher, Robert Strange. Right above: "The Yama Yama Man." In Warner's Look for the Silver Lining *(1949), June Haver imitated Ginger Rogers imitating Irene Foote imitating Bessie McCoy. Next page: Vernon and Irene rehearse in New Rochelle.*

by the studio as a technical adviser, didn't need to advise Astaire as to the dances. He set them from his memories of the Castles and their era.

The Castles' success story forms a neat precedent for Astaire-Rogers and their fame. It may be easier for us today to see the historical stresses that the film leaves out, but in 1939 most people seemed to feel that the Castle phenomenon hadn't merely recurred in the Astaire-Rogers one but had been superseded by it. Vernon and Irene first come to the attention of Elisabeth Marbury, the theatrical agent (called Maggie Sutton in the film), when they disturb her by dancing in the room above—a bit from *Top Hat.* Their personal lives are given

a high romantic gloss, and though it would have been nice to know what their marriage was really like, the gloss has its own special nostalgia and pain. Vernon's death was felt to be one of the symbolic catastrophes of the World War, and the tragic historical symmetry of 1914 and 1939 seems to grip the screen. Then, too, it was Astaire and Rogers' farewell film. The very word is like a bell. In the fadeout Vernon returns as a ghost, and then the two dancers are ghosts, twirling off down a rose-strewn path into eternity. It isn't a patch on the soul-searing exit of "Never Gonna Dance" in *Swing Time,* and *The Castles* is more like the period musicals that Fox was already turning out and would keep grinding out as show business biographies in the Forties than it is like any one of the other Astaire-Rogers films. Even the screenplay is indirectly Fox-manufactured: Richard Sherman, who wrote the final version for RKO, had written *Alexander's Ragtime Band.* Nevertheless, *The Castles* is a classic that gathers poignance with the years. It was a mating of subject and stars such as movies seldom see, and it was made at a perhaps unguessably right moment in time for both the subject and the stars. It is a very dear film.

"Waiting for the Robert E. Lee."

The Numbers. "The Yama Yama Man." From Irene Castle's autobiography *Castles in the Air:* "My greatest idol was Bessie McCoy, who was playing on Broadway in *The Three Twins,* in which she sang a song called 'The Yama Yama Man.' Bessie McCoy lived in New Rochelle and I wanted to be just like her. It took no effort to make my husky voice sound like hers and I worked very hard to copy her steps and mannerisms. The high shoulder, the way I held my hands, and anything that looked well about my dancing, I am sure I owe to the subtle grace of Bessie McCoy." Irene Castle (née Foote), doctor's daughter and New Rochelle deb, was imitating Bessie McCoy in 1909 at amateur theatricals. Five years later her "high shoulder" was an ingrained feminine attitude on the dance floors of the nation and it persisted into the Thirties—you can see a trace of it in the way Ginger Rogers dances. However, it doesn't figure in "The Yama Yama Man," a delightfully childlike routine in a clown suit with pompons. Rogers gives it a stylized extroverted interpretation that shows us both Bessie McCoy's dance and the healthy, breathless amateur who performs it. The accompaniment was recorded by Phil Ohman of Ohman and Arden, the twin-piano team that had led the pit band for Astaire's Gershwin shows.

"By the Light of the Silvery Moon" and "Who's Your Lady Friend?" Even in his solo turns Astaire doesn't dance in his own style. Vernon Castle was an "eccentric" dancer and comedian, stringy and rubber-legged. Neither in technique nor vocabulary did Astaire resemble him. As Castle he does a kind of four-square soft-shoe mixed with clog-dancing, slides and big leg-swings. None of it looks like him and yet we would never take him for anyone else.

"Only When You're in My Arms" was the one new tune written for the film and it wasn't very good. Astaire sings it as part of Vernon's proposal to Irene and it is used under the fadeout.

"Waiting for the Robert E. Lee." The Castles as a team audition for Lew Fields. If you look closely, the duets in this film are the history of the era. This is the Texas Tommy, one of the forerunners of the Lindy, and it's the kind of breezy, rambunctious dance that the Castles shortly abandoned in favor of their own more sophisticated style. At one point the dancers whip around the floor with their hands clasped at the back of each other's necks, and at another there's a surefire vaudeville effect: she leans back with her heels together (like the Klopman, A Man You Can Lean On ad); he steps over her, turns her and steps over her again.

The Castle Walk. Right: With Edna May Oliver and Clarence Derwent at the Café de Paris.

Lew Fields plays himself in the film. He was the producer and star of Vernon's first shows, half of the vaudeville team of Weber and Fields, and the father of Dorothy, Herbert and Joseph Fields.

"Too Much Mustard." The Castle Walk, say the Castles in their textbook *Modern Dancing*, "sounds silly and is silly. That is the explanation of its popularity." Irene writes: "Instead of coming *down* on the beat as everybody else did, we went up. The result was a step almost like a skip, peculiar-looking I'm sure, but exhilarating and fun to do." Today it would be called campy, but I find no camp in the Astaire–Rogers version unless it's that fresh little back kick. Maybe it was a generational difference. The number just looks infectious, like the one-step my mother and father used to do.

This sequence, at the Café de Paris, is introduced with the singing of "The Darktown Strutters Ball" by the French bandleader (French lyric by Elsie Janis). The voice on the soundtrack is that of Jean Sablon, who backed out of playing the part when he realized how small it was. (And in an even smaller part Marge Champion is seen as one of Irene's friends in the *Henpecks* sequence.)

Medley Montage. The Castles rise to fame, setting fashions and launching a nationwide dance craze with the Tango, the Polka and the Maxixe. (The Fox Trot sequence, showing the Castles with their dance instructors at Castle House, was deleted.) The Tango is strangely disappointing. It had been tamed by conservative Parisian society at *thés dansants*, and the Castles desensualized it further. The Astaire–Rogers "Castle" Tango may be correct, but it's also dull. The Maxixe is a knockout, the most infectious of all the laughter-filled dances in the film, and the most intricate. Here the Astaire–Rogers series comes full circle, for Vincent Youmans almost certainly had the Castles in the back of his mind when he wrote "The Carioca." The montage ends with the Whirlwind Tour of 1914 and the memorable shot of the Castles dancing across the country as throngs of dancing couples materialize in their wake.

Waltz Medley. The tempo is a little brisk for the Hesitation waltz, but it suits the mood of understatement in this last formal dance of the series. This is exhibition ballroom dancing at its least exhibitionistic. Dear Fred and Ginger, the world must have wondered, What are you going to do for a finish? "Oh, just a simple old-fashioned waltz." And here it is.

"Whirlwind Tour," filmed in sunlight at the RKO ranch in San Fernando Valley. The map was painted on a floor mat and the shot made from a forty-foot tower.

Production. RKO bought Irene Castle's story for Astaire and Rogers in 1936 but didn't schedule it for filming until 1938. When the movie opened in New York, Mrs. Castle, then forty-six, told Bosley Crowther in the *Times*, "I'm sure they would rather I had been dead. They even waited two years for me to kick off, I suspect, after I had sold them the story. But when they found out I was indestructible, they went ahead and made it. And I still don't feel particularly ancient."

Mrs. Castle was given approval of script, cast, direction and costumes, and she exercised it unreasonably. In her attack on the movie in *Castles in the Air*, she scores only once. Walter Ash, the Foote family servant who went with the Castles to Paris, was a Negro. RKO cast Walter Brennan. (And the film doesn't show us J. R. Europe or Ford Dabney, the Castles' very influential music directors, who were both black, nor do we see the black orchestras they led.) She implies some wide discrepancy between the film that was produced and Oscar Hammerstein's "beautiful" treatment, yet the film follows her own account of her life with Vernon in every major respect. She says that her advice on costumes was rejected, yet many of the dresses are very closely modeled on the ones she had worn in that period and she does receive a technical credit.

However, nothing seems to have enraged her more than the casting of Ginger Rogers. Schiaparelli called Rogers "the most perfect type of American woman," but she was apparently not the right type for Irene Castle. Mrs. Castle doesn't say this; she says instead, "Fred had begged me not to let her do it."

CHICAGO

NEW ORLEANS

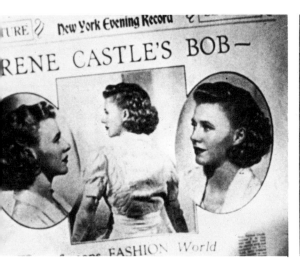

Left: The Maxixe as seen at Castles-by-the-Sea on Long Island, one of the numerous establishments that bore the Castle name. Above: Irene bobs her hair. The Castle clip was shorter than Rogers wears it in the film. Right above: Castle fashions sweep the nation.

She demanded a nationwide search *à la* Scarlett O'Hara. The studio agreed, then doublecrossed her. Miss Rogers proved impossible: she would not bob her hair or wear a wig or do without shoulder pads. Irene "nitpicked at the script and at the clothes," according to H.C. Potter. "She wanted one sequence shot over again only because Ginger, who was supposed to have just come back from riding, had no hat on, and Irene said, 'I wouldn't be caught dead riding without a hat.' And oh, the arguments and pleadings that went on about that." There happened to be an antivivisection referendum on the ballot that year in California, and soon Mrs. Castle, who was a noted animal-lover and antivivisectionist, began to hear a great deal about it from Pandro Berman's secretary. She went roaring into the campaign and the company was left to finish the film in peace.

Astaire had been her choice for Vernon, and the film had a special significance for him. He says of it: "We accomplished what we hoped for—a high-level climax to the series." But when he saw it at the Radio City Music Hall, it was evident to him that something was wrong. The sound coming across the vast distances of the theater from the loudspeakers behind the screen reached his ears a fraction of a second late—too late for Astaire. He rushed to a phone and called the studio in Hollywood. "Get someone out here right away," he said, "The film is five frames out of sync."

Below: "Who's Your Lady Friend?" Right above: The Castles fight World War One. Vernon Castle flew photo-reconnaissance over enemy lines for the British Flying Corps and was killed in a U.S. airbase crash.   Center: The last waltz.   Below: Irene gets news of Vernon's death.

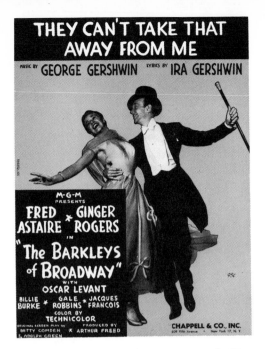

The Barkleys of Broadway

A Metro-Goldwyn-Mayer Picture released May 4, 1949

Producer **Arthur Freed** Director **Charles Walters** Associate Producer **Roger Edens** Screenplay **Betty Comden** and **Adolph Green** Musical Direction **Lennie Hayton** Orchestrations **Conrad Salinger** Vocal Arrangements **Robert Tucker** Musical Numbers Staged by **Robert Alton** "Shoes With Wings On" Staged by **Hermes Pan** Photography **Harry Stradling** Animation **Irving G. Reis** Art Direction **Cedric Gibbons** and **Edward Carfagno** Miss Roger's Gowns **Irene** Men's Styles **Valles** Hair Styles **Sydney Guilaroff** Makeup **Jack Dawn** Sound Recording **Douglas Shearer** Editor **Albert Akst** Color by Technicolor Running Time 109 minutes

Songs: Music by **Harry Warren,** lyrics by **Ira Gershwin:** "Swing Trot," "You'd Be Hard to Replace," "Bouncin' the Blues" (instrumental), "My One and Only Highland Fling," "Weekend in the Country," "Shoes With Wings On," "Manhattan Downbeat"
Music by **George Gershwin,** lyric by **Ira Gershwin:** "They Can't Take That Away From Me"

Fred Astaire *Josh Barkley* **Ginger Rogers** *Dinah Barkley* **Oscar Levant** *Ezra Millar* **Billie Burke** *Mrs. Livingston Belney* **Gale Robbins** *Shirlene* **Jacques François** *Jacques Barredout* **George Zucco** *Judge* **Clinton Sundberg** *Bert Felsher* **Hans Conreid** *Artist* **Inez Cooper** *Pamela Driscoll* **Carol Brewster** *Gloria Amboy* **Wilson Wood** *Larry*

"Manhattan Downbeat."

"Swing Trot."

The Film. In the movie-musical history books, 1949 is the year of *On the Town*. In life it was the year of *Jolson Sings Again* (the top-grossing movie of the year). The big MGM money-makers were *Neptune's Daughter* with Esther Williams; *Take Me Out to the Ballgame,* with Williams and Gene Kelly and Frank Sinatra; *In the Good Old Summertime,* Judy Garland's last movie before the collapse that led to her break with MGM, and *The Barkleys of Broadway*. These weren't great musicals and neither was *On the Town*; it was just another of the Kelly-Sinatra movies that were MGM's version of the Crosby-Astaire combination at Paramount. It was sung and danced in live or live-looking New York locations, and New York, I think, is what caused the British critics to go wild about the movie. New York had a tremendous glamor in the postwar years; I certainly felt it in *On the Town,* and every time the 20th Century Fox orchestra played "Street Scene" behind a New York stock shot, which it did constantly in that period, I would be paralyzed with desire. About that time, too, Gordon Jenkins recorded an opus called "Manhattan Towers," with narration ("It was raining the first time I saw Manhattan . . ."). That was another kick. *On the Town* made those who were susceptible to "New York, New York!" see things in it that were never there, just as *The Red Shoes* was a cultural bonanza for Americans who were starved for the magic of London and the Continent that had been cut off by the war.

The Barkleys was just another musical, too. However, it had Them, and it was raining the first time I saw Them. On a clearer day *The Barkleys* strikes me as faintly horrible in its presentation of Astaire and Rogers as "the Lunt and Fontanne of musicals," to use director Charles Walters' phrase. In the movie they play a beloved husband-and-wife musical comedy team who bicker incessantly backstage, but the Comden and Green script doesn't have the malicious wit to make us love it. As one of their satires of the temperamental glittering savages who make up show business, it isn't up to *Singin' in the Rain* or *The Band Wagon,* and in this lobby-gossip version of their own legend both Astaire and Rogers seem miscast. They weren't Alfred and Lynn and they weren't Noel and Gertie; they were the two most divinely *usual* people in the history of movies. Not by accident did they exalt commonplace settings with their poetic tap dances or detonate a ceremonious décor with their swing ballets. They were a pair of American folk dancers, glorious ones to be sure, but all their glory flowed from the fact that we could sing their songs and at least imagine ourselves doing their dances. And the reason that Rogers still looks

171

The arty playwright (Jacques François) breaks up the act.

triumphantly right with Astaire, even in this movie with so little of the old fire left, isn't just that she "gives him sex." The sexiest of his other partners, Rita Hayworth and Cyd Charisse, did very little for him. Sex unshaded by temperament isn't very interesting and, in relation to Astaire, it's useless. Rogers was not one of the great sex queens, not a "magnificent animal." She's an American classic, just as he is: common clay that we prize above exotic marble. The difference between them is that he knew it and she didn't.

Rogers always wants to be something more. Probably no other major star has so severely tried the loyalty of her public by constantly changing her appearance and her style. In 1939 she looked like her imitator, Priscilla Lane, and from then on you hardly knew what hair or eyebrows she would turn up in next, playing what kind of role. In *The Barkleys*, the team breaks up when the wife goes in for heavy dramatics. This was sly and probably irresistible, but imprudent, and the movie tries to play it both ways, first letting us think the wife is a lousy actress (a few easy laughs here), then arranging for her to have a triumph. But the dramatic "scene" that she plays to the bravos of the audience in the film is one Rogers stunt that doesn't come off—a strident, unreachably far-out impersonation of Sarah Bernhardt reciting "La Marseillaise." The bad joke is that Rogers herself is a decently accomplished serious actress, but La Rogers can almost make you forget it.

The Numbers. Fred Astaire and Ginger Rogers dancing in color to the luscious sound of the MGM orchestra: this is the way the movie opens, and no musical ever got off to a better start. We see their feet under the main title as in *Top Hat*, and then we see them, miraculously on top of the old form. The colors

172

are royal purple (the chorus) and gold (her dress), the music gleams of brass
and counteraccents, and the dance, up-tempo all the way, is one of their one-take
wonders. The number is called ''Swing Trot'' and it's the best thing in the
movie. Unfortunately, most of it has to be watched through the credits.

''You'd Be Hard to Replace.'' The songs that Harry Warren wrote in the
Forties were just as pleasing as the ones he wrote with Al Dubin for the Warner's
musicals of the Thirties. This is a warm, murmurous ballad with a sweet lyric
for Astaire to sing to Rogers. I don't care for its staging in the film—the resolution
of a love-spat, in bathrobes.

''Bouncin' the Blues.'' When I first saw *The Barkleys*, this rehearsal sequence
was the one that impressed me most because it seemed so real: the warm-
up—Rogers even does a brief barre—followed by an explosive routine that con-

*Rehearsal at the MGM Theater. Oscar Levant as friend of the family, Clinton Sundberg as an
agent, and Gale Robbins as Rogers' understudy. Levant played ''Sabre Dance''–top pop in 1949.*

"Shoes With Wings On." *With the end of the RKO series, Astaire's solos became the chief attraction, and sometimes the only attraction, of his movies. Between 1940 and 1946 he did "Say It With Firecrackers" in* Holiday Inn, *the Latin number in Adolphe Menjou's office in* You Were Never Lovelier, *"One For My Baby" in* The Sky's the Limit, *and "Puttin' On the Ritz" in* Blue Skies. *Astaire then formally retired. He came back in 1948 to replace an injured Gene Kelly in MGM's* Easter Parade. *The movie was one of the year's big hits, and a successor film was planned with the same director, Charles Walters, and co-star, Judy Garland. But before filming began on* The Barkleys of Broadway, *Garland's ill health forced her to withdraw. Ginger Rogers stepped in. On March 23, 1950, Astaire received a special Academy Award for his contributions to the musical film.*

veyed the joy that two professional dancers take in their work. But it really isn't up to "I'll Be Hard to Handle" or "Let Yourself Go," and the performance is too aggressively professional, as if to say "We old-timers can still cut it." The end is nice: he backs into the wings, beckoning her, and she pulls the curtain to cover her exit like a stripper.

"My One and Only Highland Fling," a soft-shoe duet in kilts, is a bit of dry bark off the *Brigadoon* log and not worthy of Astaire and Rogers. Yards of burred lyrics and predictable rhymes ("MacDougal-too frugal").

"A Weekend in the Country" is sung while striding down a country road, tracked by the camera. I mean no disrespect to Oscar Levant, who shares the number, when I say that it's an improvement on the "Walking the Dog" sequence in *Shall We Dance*. Astaire's walking shots were famous (Walters opened *Easter Parade* with one) and Rogers coming or going was always a pleasure to watch. It isn't dancing, but it's super walking.

"Shoes With Wings On." In the Magic Theater of Fred Astaire, this number has a high place. A witty scrambling of themes from *The Red Shoes* and "The Sorcerer's Apprentice," it has Astaire as a cobbler trying on a pair of hoofer's shoes and getting carried away among dozens of animated dancing shoes that jump down from the shelves. Wonderful things happen: the shooting gallery with the shoe line-up, Fred's kicking off the magic shoes and shooting them down, the rain of shoes that ends the number, like something out of *Alice in Wonderland*. And the vocal, sung by him in voice-over. All priceless, yet Astaire could make props come alive without the aid of trick effects, and I think I prefer those solos in which he does it—the golf dance in *Carefree*, the piano dance in *Let's Dance* with his exit riding the chairs, the metronome-and-coatrack dance in *Royal Wedding*.

"They Can't Take That Away From Me" rights the wrong committed by *Shall We Dance*, but neither the choreography nor the performance is what it might have been in 1937. The stylistic echoes—the walking side by side, the darting and swaying, the turbulence and the calm withdrawal—are so much passionless technique, and Rogers had taken on a muscular thickness in her back and arms that robs her gestures of their former beautiful transparency. It's the body of an athlete, not of a dancer. She was thirty-eight, Astaire was fifty, and the number is an old-smoothie turn. I don't think that in 1949 we could have asked for more. Why does the magic return in "Swing Trot" and

"They Can't Take That Away From Me," revived from Shall We Dance and danced by Astaire and Rogers for the first time. It was one of the numbers added to the score of The Barkleys when Rogers joined the cast.

not here? Because "Swing Trot" doesn't try for as much; it's the nature of the dance. Beauty ranks above charm. "Slowness is beauty."—Rodin.

"Manhattan Downbeat." This short, splashy finale was the 1949 version of MGM's standard "Broadway Rhythm" number, and it's just *too* standard, especially for a movie with such a snappy opening.

Production. *The Barkleys* was an unscheduled reunion with far from ideal results, but it probably wouldn't have turned out very differently if MGM had planned it from the start. "Josh" and "Dinah" still would have had His and Hers bathrooms in that cute, characterless townhouse the studio built for them to live in. Comden and Green, who were at MGM devising screenplays of *Good News* and their own *On the Town*, would almost certainly have written the script, and without a doubt this is the script they would have written. Both their vehicles for Astaire were slick and somewhat mordant variations on his career. *The Barkleys* played on his partnership with Rogers; *The Band Wagon*, on the period when, after too many bad movies, he was off the screen until *Easter Parade* brought him back. True, the songs written for *The Barkleys* might have been more inspired, but it's hard to imagine who in 1949 could have equalled "They Can't Take That Away From Me." The great age of songwriting was drawing to a close. There were very few good new songs in Astaire's movies of the Fifties. The best of these movies—*Three Little Words* and *The Band Wagon* and *Funny Face*—were built around old tunes.

Rogers, of course, hadn't made a musical in ten years (*Lady in the Dark* wasn't really a musical), although she'd done delightful little dances in some of her films—the jitterbug in *Bachelor Mother*, the Black Bottom in *Roxie Hart*, the tap dance in *The Major and the Minor*. During Astaire's low years she was at her peak—inventive, whimsical, buoyant through all her vicissitudes—until she made the one change the public wouldn't permit: she became remote and grand, first in *Lady in the Dark*, then in the Garbo role in the remake of *Grand Hotel* (called *Weekend at the Waldorf*). And then in *The Barkleys*—Sarah Bernhardt! There are people who would say that Rogers' Oscar was a kiss of death, but maybe the trouble with it was that it was presented to her by Lynn Fontanne.

At the Oscar ceremony for 1949, Fred Astaire received a special Academy Award "for his unique artistry and his contributions to the technique of musical pictures." It was presented to him by Ginger Rogers.

Off Camera

Acknowledgments

For the pictures in this book I wish to thank Eric Benson, Pandro S. Berman, The Bettmann Archive, William K. Everson, Jerome Feirman, Mr. and Mrs. Edward Glass, Lester Glassner, Herb Graff, Mr. and Mrs. Gerald Kenney, Dion McGregor, Modernage, Museum of the City of New York, New York Public Library Theater Collection, Hermes Pan, Louis Pappas, H. C. Potter, Mark Ricci, Mark Sandrich Jr., Daniel Surak, Charles L. Turner, United Press International, and Lou Valentino.

For the use of special material I am indebted to Mark Sandrich Jr. and Allan Scott.

Invaluable assistance was rendered by Arly Bondarin, Philip Chamberlain, Harris Dienstfrey, Don Knox, Clive T. Miller, Louis Pappas, Margaret Peet, Robert Sealy, and Helen Gregg Seitz.

I wish to express my gratitude to the Council of the Humanities, Princeton University, and to the John Simon Guggenheim Memorial Foundation.

Portions of this book appeared in different form in *Ballet Review*.

On the "Carioca" set. Front row: Lou Brock, Ginger Rogers, Dolores del Rio, Gene Raymond. Back: Actor Jack Goode, Raul Roulien, George Nicholls Jr., Fred Astaire, Thornton Freeland.

Camera rehearsal, "The Continental." Mark Sandrich on boom. Beneath Sandrich right to left: Dave Gould (with hat), cinematographer David Abel, assistant director Argyle Nelson (with mike). Crouching at extreme left: Hermes Pan. This is a staged publicity photograph, not an actual camera setup.

Left: With Mark Sandrich and Irving Berlin on Top Hat. *Above: With Hermes Pan, Astaire-Rogers publicity man Eddie Rubin, and Hal Borne.*

Mark Sandrich's analysis of Follow the Fleet *based on the final script of November 9, 1935, and used as a guide in production. In panels reading from top: locale of sequence, plot continuity, locale of each scene, content of each scene. Horizontal bars in the lowest panel indicate the presence of music (bottom) plus singing, dancing or novelty. Blanks indicate action and/or*

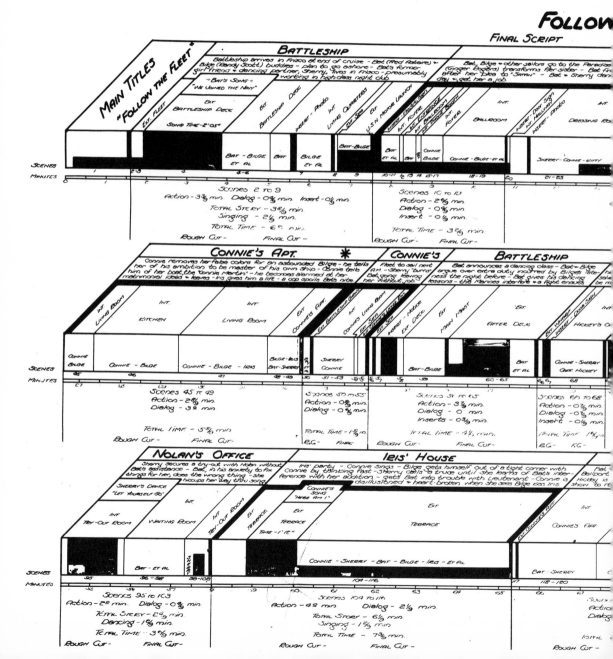

dialogue. Vertical bars are inserts and opticals (fades, wipes, dissolves). Borders bracketing sequences are heavy for night scenes, light for day. Under lowest panel: estimated running time in minutes, with totals to be compared against rough and final cuts. Sandrich also prepared comparative analyses of every film in the series.

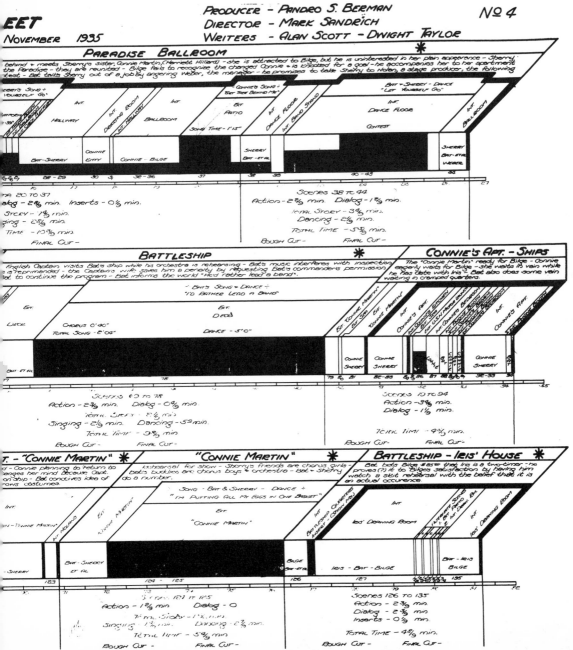

EET
November 1935

PRODUCER – PANDRO S. BERMAN
DIRECTOR – MARK SANDRICH
WRITERS – ALAN SCOTT – DWIGHT TAYLOR

№ 4

PARADISE BALLROOM

behind + meets Sherry's sister, Connie Martin, (Harriett Hilliard) - she is attracted to Bilge, but he is uninterested in her plain appearance - Sherry + the Paradise - they are reunited - Bilge fails to recognise the changed Connie + is tricked for a goal - he accompanies her to her apartment, the following deal - Bat talks Sherry out of a job by angering Weber, the manager - he promises to take Sherry to Nolan, a stage producer, the following

INT. HALLWAY / INT. DRESSING ROOM / INT. BALLROOM / EXT. PATIO / SONG TIME - 1'15" / INT. DANCE FLOOR / INT. BAND STAND / INT. DANCE FLOOR CONTEST / INT. BALLROOM

CONNIE'S SONG + "GET THEE BEHIND ME" / BAT + SHERRY - DANCE "LET YOURSELF GO"

BAT-SHERRY / CONNIE KITTY / CONNIE - BILGE / SHERRY BAT-ET-AL / SHERRY BAT-ETAL WEBER

Scenes 20 to 37
Action - 2⅔ min.   Inserts - 0⅛ min.
Story - 1⅞ min.
Singing - 2⅚ min.
Time - 13⅖ min.
FINAL CUT –

Scenes 38 to 44
Action - 2⅘ min.   Dialog - 1⅚ min.
Total Story - 3⅗ min.
Dancing - 2⅖ min.
TOTAL TIME - 5⅗ min.
ROUGH CUT –   FINAL CUT –

BATTLESHIP

English Captain visits Bat's ship while his orchestra is rehearsing - Bat's music interferes with inspection - is reprimanded - the Captain's wife saves him a penalty by requesting Bat's commander's permission - to continue the program - Bat informs the world: "I'd rather lead a band".

BAT'S SONG + DANCE + "I'D RATHER LEAD A BAND"

EXT. DECK / CHORUS 0'40" / TOTAL SONG - 6'00" / EXT. DECK / DANCE - 5'0"

BAT - ET AL

Scenes 63 to 78
Action - 2⅜ min.   Dialog - 0⅞ min.
Total Story - 8¼ min.
Singing - 2⅛ min.   Dancing - 5⅔ min.
TOTAL TIME - 9⅖ min.
ROUGH CUT –   FINAL CUT –

CONNIE'S APT. - SHIPS

The "Connie Martin" ready for Bilge - Connie eagerly waits for Bilge - she waits in vain while he has date with Iris + Bat also does some vain waiting in cramped quarters.

EXT. CONNIE MARTIN / EXT. SHIP / CONNIE MARTIN / INT. CONNIE'S APT / INT. DRESSING ROOM / INT. CONNIE'S BEDROOM / INT. CONNIE'S BEDROOM / INT. CONNIE'S APT / INT. CONNIE'S APT / STATE ROOM

CONNIE SHERRY / CONNIE SHERRY / CONNIE / CONNIE SHERRY

Scenes 79 to 94
Action - 3⅜ min.
Dialog - 1⅛ min.
TOTAL TIME - 4⅞ min.
ROUGH CUT –   FINAL CUT –

EXT. "CONNIE MARTIN"

d - Connie planning to return to - changes her mind because Capt. on ship - Bat conceives idea of rows costumes

INT. / EXT. - CONNIE MARTIN / EXT. CONNIE MARTIN / BAT ROLAND

- SHERRY / BAT - SHERRY ET AL

Scenes 103 to 105
Action - 1⅜ min.   Dialog - 0
Total Story - 1⅚ min.
Singing - 1⅓ min.   Dancing - 2⅞ min.
TOTAL TIME - 5⅘ min.
ROUGH CUT –   FINAL CUT –

"CONNIE MARTIN"

Rehearsal for show - Sherry's friends are chorus girls - Bat's buddies are chorus boys + orchestra - Bat + Sherry do a number.

SONG - BAT & SHERRY - DANCE + "I'M PUTTING ALL MY EGGS IN ONE BASKET"

EXT. "CONNIE MARTIN"

BILGE BAT-ET-AL

Scenes 123 to 125

BATTLESHIP - IRIS' HOUSE

Bat bets Bilge #25 that Iris is a two-timer - he proves (?) it to Bilge's satisfaction by having him watch a skit rehearsal with the belief that it is an actual occurrence.

INT. BATTLESHIP CHARTER MARTIN / INT. IRIS' DRAWING ROOM / INT. IRIS' DRAWING ROOM

IRIS - BAT - BILGE / BAT - IRIS BILGE

Scenes 126 to 135
Action - 2⅜ min.
Dialog - 2⅜ min.
Inserts - 0⅛ min.
TOTAL TIME - 4⅘ min.
ROUGH CUT –   FINAL CUT –

Above: Sandrich with Dwight Taylor and Allan Scott. Left: Sandrich and George Gershwin.

Ginger Rogers at her roller-skating party with actress Florence Lake, co-host Alfred Gwynne Vanderbilt Jr., Hermes Pan and Mr. and Mrs. George Murphy, March 6, 1937. Below: On the set of Shall We Dance, Pandro Berman and Ginger with Ginger mask.

Above: Jerome Kern, Dorothy Fields and George Gershwin in Hollywood, 1937.

Left: Hermes Pan rehearses Rogers.

Left: Irene Castle signs her contract with RKO in 1936, observed by Pandro Berman, George Stevens and RKO Vice President Ned E. Depinet. Stevens was initially set to direct The Story of Vernon and Irene Castle. *When it was finally filmed, in the fall of 1938, he was busy with* Gunga Din. *Right: H.C. Potter with Astaire made up as Vernon Castle in* The Henpecks.